WHAT CAUSED THE CIVIL WAR?

*Reflections on the South and
Southern History*

WHAT CAUSED THE CIVIL WAR?

REFLECTIONS ON THE SOUTH AND SOUTHERN HISTORY

EDWARD L. AYERS

W. W. NORTON & COMPANY

NEW YORK   LONDON

For information about permission to reproduce selections from this book, write to Permissions,
W. W. Norton & Company, Inc., 500 Fifth Avenue, New York, NY 10110

Manufacturing by Quebecor World, Fairfield
Book design by JAM Design
Production manager: Amanda Morrison

Library of Congress Cataloging-in-Publication Data

Ayers, Edward L., 1953–
What caused the Civil War? : reflections on the South and Southern history / Edward L. Ayers.—
1st ed.
v. cm.
Includes bibliographical references and index.
Contents: Pieces of a Southern autobiography—What we talk about when we talk about the
South—A digital Civil War—Where the North is the South—Worrying about the Civil War—
What caused the Civil War?—Exporting Reconstruction—Telling the story of the new South—In
memory of C. Vann Woodward.
ISBN 0-393-05947-2 (hardcover)
1. United States—History—Civil War, 1861–1865—Causes. 2. Southern States—History. I. Title.
E458.A98 2005
975—dc22

2005000938

ISBN-13: 978-0-393-32853-0 pbk.
ISBN-10: 0-393-32853-8 pbk.

W. W. Norton & Company, Inc., 500 Fifth Avenue, New York, N.Y. 10110
www.wwnorton.com

W. W. Norton & Company Ltd., Castle House, 75/76 Wells Street, London W1T 3QT

1 2 3 4 5 6 7 8 9 0

CONTENTS

PREFACE

I T IS hard not to have mixed feelings about the American South. To know anything about the region is to know that it is both simple and convoluted, seductive and frightening. To know the United States at the beginning of the twenty-first century is also to know that the South is of central importance to the nation and thus to the world. The region accounts for an ever-larger share of the country's population and economic growth. It has dominated the nation's politics for the last several generations, both in numbers and in values, and shows every sign of doing so for generations to come. The South's culture, black and white, has become America's culture in everything from sports to religion to music.

As a professional historian who is both a native and a longtime resident of the South, I have struggled to understand the region. I have written books about crime and punishment in the South, about the turbulent half century following Reconstruction, and about the coming of the Civil War. I have spoken with groups of

black and white teachers about ways to teach the history of segregation, with members of the Sons of Confederate Veterans about the
connection between slavery and secession, with Rotary clubs about
poverty and economic exploitation, and with Appalachian audiences about stereotypes they face. I have tried to explain the South
in California and New York, in the Netherlands, Italy, and England.
The essays that follow began with those conversations.

Three themes weave throughout the book. First, the South is
much more complicated than either its defenders or detractors
think. People of every sort have tried to simplify the South. Some
explain away the hard parts of the region's past by invoking a
sanitized heritage while others use lazy generalizations about
weather, religion, or gene pools to portray Southerners as hope-
lessly backward. Such simplifications deny the fascinating human
complexity that defines the South.

Second, old and new, past and future have intertwined throughout the South's history. Modernity has appeared in strange places
and in strange combinations. The oldest South, the South of plantation slavery, grew up as part of the most advanced economy in
the world at the time. The Confederacy stood as a remarkably
sophisticated effort at creating a brand-new nation in a matter of
months, one that waged effective war for years. Segregation was
not merely a holdover from slavery but something created anew
in the world of railroads, electric communication, and mass mer-
chandise. The latest South invokes politics and religion in the
image of an old-time world that never existed. Past, present, and
future must be untangled before we can understand any of them.

Third, we need fresh ways to think about the South. We have

fallen into habits of speech and writing that do our thinking for us, that keep us from seeing things in proportion and motion. Cliché has come to mark much of what we say about the South. The essays of this book experiment with voice, perspective, and idea to see if we might talk about the region in some new ways.

It is important to get the South right. No matter how it changes, the region will play an important role in the nation's future just as it has in the nation's past. By reflecting on the South, especially on the Civil War that defines so much of its history, we can see larger patterns. We can understand complexity, how it is that powerful events grow from intricate social processes. We can understand ambiguity, how it is that straightforward dichotomies so seldom explain social reality. We can understand the unexpected, how it is that cause and consequence so seldom seem to follow straight lines.

Pieces of a

Southern Autobiography

I T TOOK me a while to figure out that I was a Southerner. Other identities, not a few of them mistaken, dawned on me first. I had to see the South at a distance before I could see its shape and understand its power.

I was born in the mountains of North Carolina to parents who were textile mill operatives at the time. My father, Tommy Ayers, and my mother, Billie Lou Buckner, had known their days of working tobacco and hooking rugs. My father, although only twenty-one when I was born, was a veteran of the fighting in Korea. The first year of my life they lived on a farm in Micaville, North Carolina, where the red clay driveway grew so slick that my mother feared sliding into the ditch every time it rained.

When I was three, in 1956, we moved about an hour and a half north, over Iron Mountain, to Kingsport, Tennessee. There both my parents worked at the Kingsport Press, one of several industrial enterprises in the booming little city. The town had been designed from the ground up about forty years before by a number of Northern-based corporations eager to take advantage of the nearby resources, including the "Anglo-Saxon" labor force. The city fathers hired a leading city planner from Massachusetts, adopted a city manager form of government, boosted themselves to the press and investors, and prospered. Kingsport called itself the Model City and believed it. In the 1950s this Appalachian outpost was a humming, thriving place, with broad streets, a busy downtown, and high hopes. It looked to be a good place to raise a family, and so my parents came.

My parents always worked very hard. One of my first memories was riding at night in the car between shift changes—probably at eleven at night, the beginning of the graveyard shift—sitting in the backseat while Mom came into work and Dad took me back home. My mother worked at the linotype machine, my father at a printing press. I recall taking a tour and proudly watching my dad, handsome, wiry, young, and smiling, working a machine that picked up large sheets of paper and swept them high in the air. The press published complicated projects, such as the *World Book Encyclopedia*, and I spent many hours poring over the set we bought on discount, virtually memorizing the sections on "Automobiles" and admiring the layered plastic overlays that revealed complexity otherwise invisible.

When it came time to go to school, I caught the bus to Andrew Johnson Elementary. We didn't talk much about what Andrew Johnson actually did, but we knew he was a president of the United States and that he had grown up not far away from Kingsport, about thirty miles down the highway in Greeneville.

Kingsport itself had no monuments to the Civil War—or to anything else, for that matter. We seemed to have sprung from nowhere.

In the second grade I had a beautiful young teacher who led us in singing every morning. One song had acting that went along with it: "Stoop down, bend down, pick a bale of cotton." No cotton grew in East Tennessee, and I had never seen cotton plants, but the song and this teacher made it sound like fun. This teacher liked me, for we shared a high-energy level and a certain dramatic inclination. She chose me to appear with the sixth graders' glee club, putting on a big show for parents. For this show, she covered my face in burnt cork, gave me a tambourine, and made me a tall hat of white cardboard. My job, and that of Eddie Anderson at the other end of the stage, was to beat our tambourine along with the songs of the South performed by the bigger kids. At one point, under the hot lights and between songs, I took off my hat for a moment and was surprised—but pleased, I discovered—by a wave of good-natured laughter from the audience. The burnt cork stopped in a straight line across the middle of my forehead, where the hat had covered.

That would have been about 1960. So far as I know, no one at Andrew Johnson Elementary, segregated as it was, had any problems with a minstrel show. The civil rights movement must have seemed pretty far away from the white people of Kingsport at that point. The little city was about 5 percent black, the population carefully segregated. I saw black kids only rarely.

Though we lived in a Republican district in Appalachia and in a quite modern young city, the culture of white supremacy thoroughly saturated us. People I knew did not hesitate to identify bright colors as "nigger colors" and big sedans as "nigger cars." It was not uncommon to see signs that caricatured black men enjoying watermelon. Downtown, signs identified the colored entrances to the Strand and the State theaters around to the side, leading to the balcony. When we white boys fought, we charged that two on one was nigger fun; when we had to decide the last one chosen for ball, eenie meenie minie mo ended with a nigger's toe. When we wanted to frighten our younger siblings, we told them a big nigger was coming to get them. We thought nothing of it.

My family were Southern Baptists. An early photograph shows me smiling in front of a portrait of Jesus, sitting at a table with an open Bible before me, white shirt, black jacket, and black bow tie, hair neatly combed with a gentle wave on top. When I was eleven I was baptized at Litz Manor Baptist Church. I joined the Royal Ambassadors and studied my Sunday school lessons. I loved the Cub Scouts and then the Boy Scouts, also based at church. The idea of a clearly defined hierarchy of effort and accomplishment, marked by merit badges and insignia, appealed to me. I became senior patrol leader and was elected to the Order of the Arrow, an honor society that required a truly challenging "ordeal" of initiation, far off in the mountains. (I would write more of the rigors we faced, but I am pledged on my Scout's honor not to reveal any details.)

Much of this, except the minstrel show, could have happened anywhere in America in the late fifties and early sixties. But we had a sense of being different. We all knew that despite our surfer shorts, Maltese cross necklaces, and whatever other fad came and went, we were hillbillies in the eyes of the world. The Beverly Hillbillies were the stars of television then, and we recognized that the show made fun of us. Even though the show had to arrange for Jed and his clan to come from Texas so that an accidental oil discovery could set the ridiculous plots in motion, the characters talked a lot about Tennessee and had kin from there. They talked in caricatures of our accents; we knew people who said "see-ment," just the way Granny did when she talked about the "cement pond," the swimming pool. We saw that people made jokes about us—right on television—just like the way we made jokes about black people. Friends came back from vacations up North or in Florida and reported that people outside the mountains wondered if we wore shoes and had indoor plumbing.

While I was quite young, my mother went to college in Johnson City and became a much-beloved fifth-grade teacher. My father continued to work at the Kingsport Press until a strike came in the mid-1960s. A union member, Dad walked the picket line from midnight until eight in the morning and stuck with his friends as long as he could. But the fifty-dollar-a-week strike benefits didn't go far with three kids. Rather than scab he just left the press altogether. Fortunately, he had a good idea of something else he could do.

Dad became a car salesman. He could talk better than anyone I ever knew, with jokes and cussing and logic deployed in just the right measure for his audience. He specialized in used cars, which carried more profit; his business card reminded people that "Everybody Drives a Used Car." Dad worked on commission, meaning that some days he might walk the freezing or blazing lot from eight till six and not make anything, but other days he might sell three cars and be a lot of fun at dinnertime. We left the tract house where we'd lived throughout my years at elementary school and moved to a subdivision named, for no apparent reason, Colonial Heights.

NASCAR racing was the only sport in which my father was interested, and racing formed a great bond between us; we both admired Richard Petty and saw him several times at the little track outside Asheville, North Carolina, and then at the new steeply banked half-mile track in Bristol. On a vacation trip to Myrtle Beach, we stopped at Darlington, and I climbed up into the starter's box and imagined that I waved the checkered flag over the electric blue 43 car. (I liked Fireball Roberts and Rex White quite a bit too, but they drove a Ford and a Chevy respectively and we were Mopar guys, hemi guys. Dad, after all, worked at the Plymouth dealership, and we understood loyalty.)

After growing up absorbed in Scouts, Sunday school, and cars, I was hit hard by rock music in the 1960s. It was not that some slumbering talent suddenly awakened, for I could neither play nor sing; every effort at both revealed to me that my love of performance would not be satisfied by becoming the next Hendrix or Morrison. Instead, improbably enough, rock music opened to me a kind of proto-scholarship. I virtually memorized every issue of *Rolling Stone* when it came out (it seemed a lot more subversive then, printed on newsprint and boasting four-letter words and ads for drug paraphernalia), and I spent hours with my best friend poring over album covers and lyrics. That friend, Mike Harris, precociously sophisticated, taught me not to laugh at things I didn't understand. He told me about Captain Beefheart and Frank Zappa, Miles Davis and John Coltrane, music we didn't hear on the radio.

When, in English class, we were told to write a report about a poet, I immediately chose Dylan Thomas because I'd read in *Rolling Stone* that Bob Dylan had named himself after him. I went to the public library and found not only Thomas's difficult poetry but books that told me about Thomas's exciting life of drink and fallibility and that explained the poetry. I loved this—the context, the explanation, the adding of layers of meaning. I wrote a better paper than I really needed to.

My father would not countenance long hair—I knew through desperate and prolonged debate on the subject—and so, to my disappointment, I looked quite neat for the late sixties. To complete the image, I edited the student newspaper, played the role of a stuffy professor type in *Up the Down Staircase*, and was a student council leader. Underneath, however, I knew myself to be a rebel in some way I had not yet learned to express or embody. I sympathized with, identified with those who struggled for civil rights on television and those who resisted the war in Vietnam. But those struggles seemed far away from Colonial Heights and Sullivan Central High School. I switched to a friend's church, where a young pastor led honest and interesting discussions about the issues of the time.

History did not interest me. It was just a boring textbook and a dull coach, a wasted hour. I lived four miles from the great Warrior's Path of the American Indians, five miles from a TVA dam, ten miles from a place Daniel Boone had hunted, and within easy driving distance of the Cumberland Gap, the coalfields, the haunts of Parson Brownlow, the center of Southern abolitionism, and all the other wonders of my fascinating part of the country. I was oblivious of it all. I cared nothing about, and knew nothing of, the Civil War that had so divided East Tennessee.

Though I loved to hike and camp in the mountains, my friends and I laughed at country music and had no idea that we went to high school fifteen miles from the birthplace of that music. We liked it when the Byrds or Dylan did country, but the real stuff we saw on Saturday afternoon TV—Porter Wagoner with Dolly Parton in shiny outfits and bouffant hair—struck us as everything we wanted to leave behind. We were children of the Age of Aquarius, citizens of the world, open to sitars and African drums, distrustful and disdainful of the politics, style, and accents of the culture all around us. Some kids we went to school with belonged to that culture in ways we did not. I remember one friend, a quiet towheaded boy, singing "Wildwood Flower" one day at recess, pronouncing "hair" just like Mother Maybelle Carter. He was amazed that I'd never heard of the song.

Despite my obtuseness, I had long been unintentionally preparing for what became my life's calling. The most memorable place of my childhood was the home of my paternal grandparents, Fred and Dell Ayers. They lived in Yancey County, North Carolina, where my parents had grown up, high in the mountains. They had long enjoyed running water and an indoor bathroom, but they heated the house with a coal stove that my grandmother had to keep filled one bucket at a time from the woodshed. They did not have a telephone until I was fifteen. The road out front was dirt and, to my grandmother's persistent annoyance, supplied a never-ending cloud of dust that worked its way through the screen door.

My grandmother had been born in that house (built during the Civil War, I was told) back in 1897, and she and my grandfather had moved there in the late 1920s after a brief time in West Virginia. My grandfather (Paw, I called him) used to joke about how run-down the place had been when they moved in; the briars had grown so thick, he said, that the rabbits had to wear leather jackets. Fred Ayers was funny and sly, a carpenter and a rounder. He was gone from home for months at a time, working on big building projects up in Washington, D.C. When he returned home, he chafed at the limitations of the farm. He gambled and drank and would come home late, loud and mean. I hid his liquor because I hated him when he was drunk and tormented my grandmother.

Dell Ayers—Grandmaw—was about five feet tall but tough. She could bully cows through gates and snap the heads off chickens. I loved her deeply, and we spent a lot of time together while my grandfather was gone. I would stay at her house for weeks at a time in the summer. She spoiled me, letting me sleep late and then watch cartoons and the Three Stooges on the one channel they received on their black-and-white television. She made my favorite apple pies and biscuits. She would walk with me all over the steep hills of the farm, going to the blackberry patch, showing me the origins of the spring, climbing high to look down on Cane River.

At night, after watching whatever was on ABC (it was strange to see *The Jetsons* in such a setting), we read the Bible together. She especially loved Revelation, which scared the dickens out of me with its images of the apocalypse and retribution for sins large and small. We'd go to bed early, and I would lie there imagining Jesus descending through the moonlit clouds and the dead arising from the family cemetery up on top of the hill. I worried about the Matchbox car I had taken from one of my friends. I also worried about whether Paw would get to go to heaven with us when the Day of Judgment came.

On Sunday Grandmaw and I went to Riverside Baptist Church. She couldn't drive, so we would have to hope a neighbor would stop by. One time Paw took us. He got up, shaved, put on his nice blue double-breasted suit, parked his truck in front of the church, and then leaned conspicuously against the front fender, reading the Asheville paper while others walked by into church.

The church was something very different from what I saw back in Colonial Heights. At home, everything was decorous and organized. At Riverside, people sometimes cried and talked in tongues. In the singing, I joined in with the other males on the echoing lines in the hymns, imagining that I was hitting profound bass notes. And I remember shaking hands with one of Grandmaw's friends and her comment when she noticed no calluses. "You aren't a farm boy, are you?" she asked kindly.

I was not. Whenever I visited Grandmaw and Paw, I felt a deep connection to the place. I knew every stretch of the creek, every corner of the barn, smokehouse, and corncrib. I handled every old tool in the woodshed and every object and scrap of paper in the cabinets around the houses. I fooled around in the fields, picking a few worms off the tobacco and stacking a few tobacco sticks.

I went fox hunting with my grandfather, sitting around the fire at the campsite, listening to the dogs chase across the ridges as they bayed in excitement and anticipation.

But I was not a farmer. I did not really belong in Burnsville. Living with an elderly lady, I imagined that the whole county was like that, behind the times. I had a wonderful aunt and uncle who lived in town, and they had a boy just one year younger than I was. He played Little League and had several channels on his TV and visited Asheville. But he did talk a little different from me and didn't live in Kingsport, where we had a McDonald's. I pictured us as farther apart than we really were. I suspect that he played up the difference too, amusing himself with his cousin who knew so little about country life.

To me, Burnsville stood for my family's past. It was close enough to visit yet far enough away to embody things abandoned. In this it was no different from the grandparents' farms of many of my generation of Southerners. It showed us how far we had come, how quickly things had changed. But that farm did not feel like "history." It was associated with no events, no public acknowledgment. It was just there, fading before our eyes, a lost America. I didn't know what to do with it, so I just held it close to my heart but away from any future I imagined for myself.

That future, I thought in some vague way, might involve writing. I got a job in a local bookstore when I was sixteen, working for $1.80 an hour. Straightening up the paperbacks and taking them with me to lunch or even home in the evenings, not bending the covers, I learned of Norman Mailer and Philip Roth, of Saul Bellow and Tom Wolfe, of the *Whole Earth Catalog* and the *I Ching*, of Kurt Vonnegut and Richard Brautigan. I also found, in the classics section, William Faulkner and Thomas Wolfe. I read at every chance and couldn't wait for college.

The University of Tennessee lay about ninety minutes away in Knoxville. I, along with all my friends, intended to go there. The university had open admissions and was virtually free, so there was really no great suspense or deliberation. I applied nowhere else. UT was big and had whatever I would need, I felt sure. I spoke to a reporter at the local newspaper, and he steered me away from journalism school. He told me that I could learn to write in lots of majors, that I should instead study a subject so that I would have something to say. I decided that American Studies would do the trick, since it was basically a disciplined version of what I was studying anyway in *Rolling Stone* and on record jackets and in the borrowed paperbacks. I wanted to be Tom Wolfe, offering hip commentary on the America around me. And the back of *The Kandy-Kolored Tangerine-Flake Streamline Baby* told me he had a Ph.D. in American Studies.

The university in 1971 was hazy with pot smoke, loud music, and too many kids loose for the first time in big concrete dorms. In my very first quarter I found my calling. I somehow ended up taking Honors Western Civilization with a famous young professor on campus, Richard Marius. He blew me away. He had grown up in East Tennessee and had gone to UT before attending Yale Divinity School and then graduate school at Yale in history. He knew everything in every language and in every time, it seemed. He wrote learned biographies on Martin Luther and Thomas More, but he had also just published a novel set in our very own

East Tennessee in the nineteenth century. The book was out in paperback and looked just like the books of Bellow's and Mailer's and Roth's and Wolfe's, with exuberant reviews on the back. To make it all even better, Marius wrote a weekly editorial for the student newspaper in which he attacked the war in Vietnam and silly university policies.

I craved whatever it was that Richard Marius possessed, whatever spark that fired him. Over the next three years I pursued the alluring, if vague, goal of being a professor, a professor of American Studies. I took mainly literature and confined my United States history to the twentieth century. I was more interested in sociology, philosophy, art history, and economics than in history.

It never occurred to me to study the South. The South, certainly of the nineteenth century, possessed none of the things that had drawn me to academic life in the first place, the rich cultural stew of books, ideas, and music. It seemed to me to be defined by poverty and injustice, by its very lack of history. I did find James Agee fascinating, for he had lived on my very street in Knoxville, and he had written fiction, journalism, and film criticism before dying young. As for the earlier stuff of the South, what was there to study? In the meantime, while I was a freshman and barely nineteen, my number came up high for the last draft for Vietnam. History had passed me by again, just as it had with civil rights and the summer of love. I seemed a few years late for everything interesting.

In the summer between my second and third years at UT I worked for a carnival. I lived in my car for an entire summer and worked on the Sky Wheel, a double Ferris wheel. I carried a box of paperback novels with me and felt pretty sure that I was living as Jack Kerouac would have lived. I had never been north of the Tennessee line, and this carnival took me through Delaware, Maryland, New York, and Pennsylvania. The work was hard, but I enjoyed running the ride with loud eight tracks of Steppenwolf and the Doobie Brothers blasting from enormous speakers twelve hours a day as I "bucked tubs"—loaded riders.

I had worked every day but two for the entire summer when a new friend of mine, Clyde, a young black guy from Flint, Michigan, and I played hooky from the carnival in Buffalo to go see Niagara Falls. The docked pay was worth it. Clyde and I got pulled over for no particular reason, and the policeman, looking at my Tennessee driver's license, commented that I would not be riding around with a black boy back home, now would I? Clyde became my best friend in the carnival, and he introduced me to the music of Al Green, who soon started singing from the big speakers on the Sky Wheel.

On the way home from the carnival I went out of my way to visit New Haven and Yale University. A professor at UT had told me it was the best place for American Studies and, just as important, Tom Wolfe's Ph.D. in American Studies had come from Yale. And of course Richard Marius had gone there.

Yale appeared to be everything I thought it would be. I was unabashed when a couple of students walking their Irish setter in their blazers advised me, after a few minutes of conversation in which I told them that I was hoping to talk with the head of the American Studies program the next day, that I might want to clean up my act a bit beforehand, that I looked like Huckleberry

Finn. I'm sure I did. I had a Carlos Santana halo of hair, uncut all summer, and Neil Young sideburns. I had a dark tan and had been living in a car. I was probably pretty rough-looking, even if I did blow enough money to stay at the Holiday Inn that night.

The next morning I sat nervously waiting for the chairman of the American Studies Program. The Hall of Graduate Studies looked just like *The Paper Chase*, a recent movie about Harvard Law School starring a young actor to whom I imagined I bore a resemblance. The walls were covered with dark oak, and the windows looked like those in a cathedral (I assumed, never having seen one); copies of *American Quarterly* were stacked next to the chair where I waited. I was pretty sure I didn't belong in such a place.

When Professor Sydney Ahlstrom arrived, I was a little surprised. He had recently won a National Book Award for his *A Religious History of the American People*, but he didn't look much like what I had expected. No pipe, no elbow patches. Instead, he was about five and a half feet tall, with a crew cut, plaid shorts, sandals with socks, and a plastic daisy on his briefcase. Professor Ahlstrom was kind but said about all he could say to a guy who showed up from Tennessee with wild hair, no prior warning, and no record to present: Do very well in your courses, get good letters of recommendation, and a good GRE (whatever that was), and we'll be happy to look at your file.

Back at UT I met my future wife, Abby Brown. After I graduated from UT the next summer, Abby and I married within weeks of finishing my courses. She was going to get her master's degree in Johnson City, at East Tennessee State, where my mother and sister had gone for their degrees. Freshly armed in the middle of a bruising recession with a B.A. in American Studies, twenty-one and looking even younger, I wasn't counting on much of a job in Johnson City. Sure enough, I worked in the credit department of a local tire store and in a factory putting electric heaters in boxes.

But I got a position I applied for at the state employment agency, the director of the Johnson City Youth Center. My job was to recruit "problem youth" to the center (a concrete block shell of a building) and then steer them to job training (which never appeared). I did the first part very well. All it took was free food collected from a local bakery, free pool, free Ping-Pong, free basketball, and free music. Abby helped me paint the place, and I had a poster printed: "No Hassle, No Bull, Just a Place to Be." We soon had a regular group of kids, black and white, male and female. I spent most of my time hanging out with them, learning more about crime, neglect, dysfunction, and broken self-image than I wanted to know. Two kids who had just gotten married, neither of them yet eighteen and both afraid to go home, came to the youth center as the best place they could think of to celebrate. I also learned that such kids could be smart, funny, hopeful, and willing to work hard. Labels didn't seem to fit very well.

In the meantime I sent in my applications to graduate school and read everything I thought might be useful, from Edgar Allan Poe to Daniel Boorstin to Thomas Pynchon. I systematically worked my way through decades of *American Quarterly*, a profoundly disorienting experience that left me sure that I knew absolutely nothing. Despite my ignorance, Yale took me and even offered a fellowship. I was thrilled, of course, not realizing just how unlikely it was that they were admitting me.

Abby finished her degree that spring of 1975, and we loaded up a U-Haul and drove to New Haven. My father helped us drive up on the interstate, and his first words after we had found our way to the married student housing complex near the abandoned Olin plant were: "I wouldn't live here for a million dollars. I'll drive the truck if you want to head back home." We didn't, and we soon began to settle in.

Overnight Abby and I became Southerners. People continually commented on our accents, and some professed not to be able to understand us. Abby ordered a lemonade our first day in New Haven, and the man behind the counter, puzzled, said, "Ham and eggs?" When an Israeli couple across the hall had us over for dinner along with a couple from Ohio, the Ohio folks asked the Israelis if they could hear any difference in our accents. In all friendliness, the Israelis acknowledged that they could indeed because "we watch *Hee Haw* all the time." We smiled weakly. Abby and I decided to make the best of the situation. It was easy to traffic in imagined exoticism at dinners with our friends, and I must admit I did, telling every colorful story I could conjure. Many of them were largely true.

But I still did not want to study the South. I noted that the students ahead of me whom I most admired were advisees of David Brion Davis. Professor Davis had been on leave my first year, but I had heard over and over again of his brilliance. He had come to Yale not long before, and his overwhelming *The Problem of Slavery in the Age of Revolution* had just won the Pulitzer Prize. My classmates and

I, along with everyone else who read the book, were in awe. In ways I did not understand at the time, my entire view of history took shape from the *Problem of Slavery*. David Davis showed how the big structures of ideology wove into the big structures of economy and state and how all of it could change. He made it clear that history and complexity are synonymous. And he showed us that moral clarity did not demand moral simplicity. Though relatively young, self-effacing, and exceedingly kind, David Davis had a full dark beard and seemed as imposing as any intellectual I could imagine. We could find no label to define him. I determined that I had to work with him, whatever my dissertation might be about.

In the meantime, C. Vann Woodward, the most eminent of all Southern historians, was retiring, and I signed up for his class on the New South, the last class he was to teach. I knew almost nothing of Southern history, and most of the other students in the class had already worked together for a semester on the Old South. Woodward was reserved, weary of the battles of academic life, it seemed, and grieving for a son lost to cancer at twenty-one, but the books he assigned crackled with life. None burned with more energy than his own *Origins of the New South*, written twenty-five years earlier. There was no need to study fiction to read literature, I decided; this was history *as* literature. Professor Woodward was kind to me but took no special interest in this kid from Tennessee. He had seen generations of Southern white boys come through Yale, all imagining that they were the first to reckon with regional difference.

Visiting my grandparents during graduate school, full of a new self-awareness of the Southern history all around me, I was stunned when my grandfather casually referred to an ancient apple tree on the place as Kizzie's tree. *Roots* had been the rage on television in 1977, but he had not seen it. In *Roots*, Kizzie was the daughter of Kunta Kinte, the lead character, a first-generation African American. I asked Paw why he called the tree by that name. He told me that "back in slave time, a nigger woman named Kizzie took apples from this tree and hid them in the straw in the barn for her children."

I couldn't believe it. Slaves had lived here, on this mountain farm? "Well, of course." Paw scoffed at his overeducated grandchild. "Who do you think cleared all this land? Your grandmaw's people were big slaveholders." The pieces did not fit. What was slavery doing here, in the highest Appalachians? I had imagined that my family had lived above the worst of Southern history, or at least outside it. I had taken pride in their rugged self-reliance. Now, like some fake Faulkner character, I discovered complicity in the great sin of the South. Genealogical research revealed five pages of slaveholders in Yancey County, and I recognized some familiar names among them, but the exact degree of complicity remained for me to imagine. Given our subsequent lack of family wealth, I believe my grandfather may have exaggerated. But the impact had already been made.

During that same trip to Burnsville, some of the so-called Florida people, who were building small houses in the mountains for the summers, came to visit. Paw liked working for them. One family of Floridians drove up the dirt road in a huge RV, and as soon as they got out, I could see they had come on an anthropological mission. The father had told his wife and children about this colorful old mountain man who was building their vacation house for them. The kids, teenagers, made no effort to hide their amusement at everything they saw around them: the unpainted and rusty tin roof, the old pictures on the walls, the accents and vocabulary of my grandparents. The visitors patronized their elderly hosts shamelessly. Sitting in the living room, they ignored me for a while, but the mother eventually turned to me and asked where I lived. "New Haven, Connecticut," I answered, in a modulated version of the same accent as my grandparents. Surprised, and with the other family members suddenly listening, she asked what I was doing there. "Studying at Yale," I said.

I had spoiled the expedition. I was furious at the visitors' casual and undeserved arrogance, their disdain for a culture I understood even if I did not fully share, and my own similarities to them. I did not reflect on what it said about me that I cared about what these strangers thought of me. But I did now know what I had come to expect: I wanted to write about the South.

Back in New Haven, David Davis kindly agreed to advise my dissertation and asked what I was thinking of writing about. I told him that I wanted to do Southern crime and prisons. Everyone had heard of Southern dueling, lynching, moonshining, chain gangs, and the like; I could explain this topic to my parents, and they might see why somebody would want to write about that. I composed a proposal based largely on a few vague references to potential sources.

When I picked up my proposal from the departmental secretary, she informed me that it had been approved but that the committee doubted that I would find any of the sources I was looking for. That was alarming, for Abby had decided to take the summer off from her teaching job at the Gesell Institute Nursery School, a job that was sustaining us, and travel with me to archives across the South in a youthful adventure. We bought a tent and a propane grill from Sears and were preparing to live in Kampgrounds of America (KOA, we soon decided, stood for Kamping on Asphalt) for five dollars a night in Jackson, Montgomery, and Nashville. While in Atlanta we would sponge off Abby's sister and brother-in-law, wonderful people who had previously been two of our best friends. We hoped the friendship would endure weeks of eating their food and getting in their way.

After many dramas of weather and poverty and heat as well as of archival discovery, I began to learn where to look to find the sort of material I was searching for. I researched for another year, returning to Atlanta for weeks. I taught myself statistics from a textbook and videotapes. I taught myself how to use the imposing mainframe computer. I wrote furiously on the typewriter (one of the last graduate students to do so, in all likelihood) and barely filled enough paper to apply for jobs in the fall of 1979.

I suddenly realized that writing about the South had turned me into a Southern historian as far as the job market was concerned, whether I wanted to be one or not. I could not claim to be a cultural or an intellectual historian, by the logic of the profession, because I studied the South. I had defined myself as a Southern historian even though I knew profoundly little about the region, just what I had learned in one course and in writing my dissertation. As it turned out, there was only one job in Southern history that year, at the University of Virginia. Calculating the odds, I worried that I'd be back to stapling boxes for electric heaters or working up credit reports.

I was invited to fly down to Charlottesville for an on-campus visit. (I did not tell my interviewers that this would be my first airplane flight.) As soon as I saw the University of Virginia, I loved the place. It seemed to combine Tennessee and Yale, public and private, Southern and cosmopolitan. I felt right at home on the hilly Piedmont landscape, the Blue Ridge hovering in the distance. Kingsport and our families lay only four hours away down I-81. I got the job and raced to finish my dissertation before the teaching began. I mailed the manuscript to New Haven on my first day of class in September 1980.

Hired to teach Southern history, I had no choice but to grow into a Southern historian. Fortunately, I loved teaching, which seemed to combine the inherited traits of my conscientious mother and my fast-talking father. Fortunately too I developed a deep and abiding fascination with all parts of Southern history, things that had never interested me before. Teaching the history of the South to descendants of the Southern aristocracy and descendants of slaves as well as to the many Northerners and non-Americans at UVa revealed to me the power of Southern history.

As I lectured year after year about slavery, Reconstruction, and the New South, I came to see new layers of meaning in those stories. As I read hundreds of undergraduate papers and dozens of doctoral dissertations, I learned of the many untold stories of the South. As I lived among the battlefields and monuments of the Civil War, I came to feel their pull. As Abby and I raised our children in the Virginia countryside, on a road where enslaved people and Confederates, farm wagons and hot rods had traveled, I felt an ever-deepening connection to those who had lived here before.

The South is more interesting than I ever imagined growing up there. To atone, I have tried in various ways to capture the richness and complexity of the Southern past and present. I have experimented with storytelling, with digital archives, with inspiration from other disciplines, and with perspectives from living abroad. The essays that follow chart those experiments.

WHAT WE TALK ABOUT WHEN
WE TALK ABOUT THE SOUTH

G IVEN ALL that has been written and said about the South, we might expect that Americans would be able to think clearly about the region. Yet television, movies, novels, roadside markers, old history books, and jokes tell the same basic stories about the South over and over, even when people know these stories are not true to their own experiences or to the complexity of human life. Southerners know that when they meet people from other places those non-Southerners know the stories too—and believe some of them. One Virginian who went to Harvard in the early 1980s fantasized about putting a sign around his neck to foreclose some of the questions he repeatedly faced or imagined he faced: " 'Yes, I am from the South. No, I do not know your uncle in Mobile. No, I was not born there. Both of my parents, in fact, are literate. No, I do not like Molly Hatchet. No, I do not watch *Hee Haw*. No, I do not own slaves. No, I do not want any. Thank you very much. Have a nice day.' " He concluded that the sign strategy would not work, though, "because everyone would think someone else had written it for me, probably so I wouldn't have to memorize it."[1]

Geographers have noted that Americans, with remarkable uniformity and consistency, picture their country's regions in ways that blur their diverse human characteristics into stereotypes. One of the chief features of that imagined map is the Southern Trough, which cuts across Mississippi and Alabama, embracing parts of Arkansas, Louisiana, and Georgia at its edges. This trough appears to most Americans as the least desirable place in the United States in which to live. Other Southern states cannot take too much grim comfort from such disparagement of their deep South neighbors, for the sides of the trough rise only gradually until they reach the usual boundaries of what Americans take to be the North, the Midwest, and the West. The whole South appears to be a vast saucer of unpleasant associations.[2]

Polls tell us, however, that white Southerners are the Americans most satisfied with their home states. In their eyes, the Southern Trough is a sheltered valley, shielded from the most corrosive effects of Yankee greed and rudeness. These white Southerners believe they live in the best part of the United States. People from elsewhere in the country look down on Southerners, they believe, only because these other Americans do not really know the South and its residents.[3]

Things are especially complicated for black Southerners. "It seems very often that blacks in the North feel themselves superior to blacks in the South," Eddy Harris, a non-Southern black man, reported, "because they think blacks in the South were simple-minded enough to stay and suffer the worst of the horrors and indignities. Southern blacks too often are called 'Bamas' and country niggers, and are seen as backward and uneducated." But Southern blacks are just as confident as their white neighbors that non-Southerners just don't get it. As an African Southerner told Harris, "blacks in the South look down on blacks in the North. 'They're up there killing each other, doing the white man's work,' he said. 'They escaped to the Promised Land and got handed a bunch of lies. Now they don't know what to do.'" The South, by contrast, appears at least knowable, predictable. Many Northern blacks see in the South the foundation for their own virtues and a return to those virtues as the best hope of beleaguered Northern communities.[4]

Perhaps reflecting such views, the tide of black migration has turned. For decades after slavery, black Southerners escaped the South at the first opportunity; now many more blacks are moving to the South than are leaving. All top five destinations for migrating black Americans are Southern cities. Eddy Harris, after traveling throughout the South, came to wonder if he had not been wrong about the region: "I tried to remember why I had come to the South in the first place, what I had expected to find. White people shooting at me. Black people bitching and moaning. A reason to hate this place. Or was I looking for a reason to love this place? I really didn't know anymore." Harris found himself asking the question many black Americans have apparently asked themselves: What "irrational love" of the South "have I inherited, do I harbor and long to admit? In what weird ways is the South not just an ancestral home, but my home as well? How much of this place is within me?"[5]

Some African Americans have found, to their surprise, that the South exerts the emotional pull of a homeland, more palpable and credible than an Africa whose landscape and language they do not know. The South has always had a different moral geography for blacks and whites; its history has always had a different trajectory. Black Southerners have not loved "the" South as it has been symbolized so frequently; no flags, monuments, or anthems have connected black Southerners with the official South. But black Americans have made parts of Southern states their own through sweat and sacrifice; they have loved certain farms, houses, and streets. The South for these Southerners is a place to love and a place to hate, a place impossible to figure out.[6]

As the South's defenders claim, it is not easily understood by outsiders; as its critics claim, it is apparently not understood much better by its resident defenders. The South has suffered from generalizations that trivialize it, whether those generalizations take the form of romantic and nostalgic dreams of the past, arrogant regional stereotypes, or scholarly arguments about central themes and unifying characteristics. Positive or negative, these images of the South keep us from seeing the people of the region with the fullness and empathy all people deserve.

Polls show us that Americans from all over the country picture the South as looking backward. From the positive point of view, Southerners seem to respect the past, the land, and their elders. From the negative point of view, the South appears to be dominated by nostalgia and dullness. These images are different sides of the same coin, different aspects of the basic story we tell ourselves about the South: It is the American place where modern life has not fully arrived, for good and for ill.

People have not merely made up this story from whole cloth. There can be no doubt that the South has been poorer than the rest of the country, less technologically advanced, more wedded to racial exploitation and segregation. But when it is portrayed as a "culture" or "society," even a "civilization," that stands as the binary opposite of the North, a relative situation tends to become an absolute characteristic; Southern differences with the North are transformed into traits that mark the very soul of the Southern people. Even the most original historian of the relationship between the South and the nation argued that students of the region "should not be concerned indiscriminately with everything that occurs within the South" but should focus only at those "points where the conditions of the Southern region differ from those of other regions." This assumption underlies much of Southern studies. Without obvious and clearly demarcated difference, it appears, there is no justification for Southern history.[7]

People realize that when they speak of "Southern culture," they are creating a fiction, an image of a geographically bounded and coherent set of attributes to be set off against a mythical non-South. Accordingly, people try to introduce complexity by qualifying the idea of the South, pointing out that the mountains are different from the lowlands, that whites are different from blacks, men from women, rich from poor. Often those who speak with the greatest conviction about the reality of a Southern culture are those who most emphasize its internal diversity. Yet the very language of "Southern culture" suggests that there are hidden ligaments and tissues holding it all together in some way.

Anthropologists, from whom historians over the years have borrowed the notions of culture as systems, things, templates, and possessions, have recently warned us to quit thinking in these metaphors. As soon as we speak of cultures, they point out, we begin to "essentialize," as the jargon has it, to locate in some other people an essence of what they really are; to "exoticize," to focus on and exaggerate the difference between one's self and the object of contemplation; to "totalize," to make "specific features of a society's thought or practice not only its essence but also its totality." We draw boundaries between things we call cultures and then fill in those boundaries with something to make them meaningful.[8]

Americans believe, hope the South is different and so tend to look for differences to confirm that belief, that "knowledge." White Southerners are, until proved otherwise, traditional, backward, obsessed with the past, friendly, potentially violent, racist, and polite. Black Southerners are, until evidence is presented to the contrary, more friendly and down-home than their Northern counterparts, more conservative and religious. When Southerners do not behave in these ways, they are deemed less Southern, less fitted to the place where they live, exceptions. Some see such people as more cosmopolitan, others as Yankee wanna-bes, ashamed of what should be their real identity.

The South plays a key role in the nation's self-image: the role of evil tendencies overcome, of mistakes atoned for, of progress yet to be made. Before it can play that role effectively, it has to be set apart as a distinct place that carries certain fundamental characteristics. As a result, Southern difference is continually being re-created and reinforced. Americans, black and white, somehow need to know that the South is different and so tend to look for differences to confirm that belief. This is not something that is only done to the South by malevolent, insensitive non-Southerners. The North and the South have conspired to create each other's identity as well as their own. The South eagerly defines itself against the North, advertising itself as more earthy, more devoted to family values, more spiritual and then is furious to have things turned around, to hear itself called hick, phony, and superstitious. The South feeds the sense of difference and then resents the consequences of difference.

Southerners with something to sell traffic in difference, eagerly market any distinctiveness they can claim—especially now that the Southern black freedom movement and the spread of racial conflict in the North and West have made the South seem less uniquely repugnant. Culture is a great natural resource: It is as renewable as trees, as deep as mines. Each state has found its singular vein. Virginia quarries its Jeffersonian period, while Georgia sells burning Atlanta, Mississippi and Alabama fight over which is the deeper South, Tennessee offers country music while Kentucky tenders bluegrass and Louisiana hawks Cajun. North Carolina even has a vaguely Orwellian-sounding branch of government called the Department of Cultural Resources. There is, accordingly, an unmistakable tendency for so-called cultural traits to coincide with state boundaries. Notice the architecture of the welcome stations along the interstates, with white columns at the portals of South Carolina and Mississippi, eighteenth-century plantation houses when you enter Virginia, and log cabin themes when you roll into Tennessee a few hundred yards away. Think of the names of state university athletic mascots: Cavaliers, Rebels, Volunteers—all rich with (white) historical connotation, all accentuating the differences at the state lines.[9]

The South needs these internal differences. With tourism as one of its major industries, the South, like other places, needs as much diversity as it can be made to contain, as many subregional cookbooks as it can produce, as many license plates and gimme hats, as many institutes, journals, encyclopedias, and historians. A considerable portion of what we see as Southern culture is manufactured to order. People want to manage, enhance, manufacture memory, to be a part of something larger than themselves. Throughout the modern era, traditions have been invented on the spot—the kilt, for example, or Betsy Ross—giving a satisfying pedigree to something that is in fact much newer or more ad hoc. The idea of the Old South was in some ways a sales job in the first place, given that at the time of the Civil War many of the plantation districts of Mississippi, Texas, and Arkansas were no older than many of today's subdivisions. Now, in turn, new places often try to distill an essence of the imagined old ones, with shopping centers wearing the regalia of plantations, with housing developments dressed as old villages.[10]

I once visited my grandparents in their small town in the mountains of western North Carolina. On that Saturday the town square was filled with a mountain crafts fair. People lined up to try the apple butter simmering in the iron kettle, to watch the dolls dance on the board, to watch the quilters, to listen to the fiddle music. I had no time to dawdle, since my grandparents were waiting for me, so I stopped in for a fast burger at the new Hardee's on the bypass. Being Southern, I automatically made conversation with the young woman behind the counter as she filled my order. "Nice craft fair," I imaginatively offered. "Yeah, I guess," she said in her mountain accent as she poured the sweetened iced tea into the cup emblazoned with the corporate logo. "Have you ever seen so many Yankees in your life?" Sure enough, I noticed when I dropped in later, the cars parked all around the square were likely to be from Pennsylvania, Florida, or New York. In fact, upon examination, it appeared that many of the authentic artisans were also Yankees, or at least yuppies. The crafts may have been of authentic Appalachian style, celebrating the mountain heritage (the name of the county's high school), but the people in the overalls and gingham were not. Exactly where authenticity resided in this episode was not clear to me then, nor is it now. A good case could be made for both sides—and neither.

It seems only commonsensical that an older culture that has somehow managed to persist into the present is on the verge of fading away. The bucket of Southern distinctiveness, it appears, was full up to the brim in 1865 but has been leaking faster and faster ever since. The experience of those who live now in the South, with its confusion, complications, and compromises, seems not as fully Southern as the society that came before, one that appears more unified and coherent. The lovingly re-created models of log cabins, plantation homes, forts, and villages that dot the South try to recapture the authentic history, one untainted by time, change, or contact with the outside world. Today's experiences of Wal-Mart, country radio, and NASCAR, by contrast, seem somehow less organically related to the region, the products of infection by mass communication and business.

Ironically, though, Southerners have always held similar fears. For as long as people have believed there was a South they have also believed it was disappearing. Virginians and Carolinians thought it was dying as early as the 1830s, with too much easy money in the Cotton Kingdom pulling people to raw places, such as Alabama and Mississippi, that knew nothing of true Southern gentility. Then people felt certain that the South would be erased by the end of slavery or Reconstruction. People held every expectation that the South would not survive the effects of automobiles or radios, of World War II and the postwar bulldozer revolution. There was reason to believe that the events of *Brown v. Board of Education*, Montgomery, Greensboro, Selma, and Birmingham might kill off the South. If that did not do the trick, surely the inexorable spread of strip malls, fast-food places, cable and satellite dishes marked the end of the South.[11]

From its very beginning, people have believed that the South was not only disappearing but also declining, defined against an earlier South that was somehow more authentic, real, more unified and distinct. Jefferson's South declined into the delusion of Calhoun's South, which declined into the incompetence of Jefferson Davis's South, which declined into the corruption of the carpetbaggers' South, which declined into the poverty and inbreeding of Faulkner's South, which declined into the race baiting of George Wallace's South, which declined into the scandals of Jim Bakker and Jimmy Swaggart. The South has always seemed to live on the edge of extinction, the good as well as the bad perpetually disappearing. A writer recently pleaded with his fellow Southerners to realize that "all our strengths—of family and history and tradition, of geography and climate, of music and food, of spoken and written language—are endangered treasures."[12]

But the South, perpetually fading, seems also perpetually with us. Sociologists have measured the shape and depth of Southern distinctiveness, finding that the perception of it does not disappear as we might expect, that education and contact with the non-South actually heighten Southern self-consciousness. People apparently need to be able to think in spatial terms, to identify various facets of "national character" with various places within the nation, to find people who embody some set of traits that others find especially attractive or—more often—repellent or problematic. Americans of course are not alone in this need; throughout the world, people tend to divide national character along various lines—often a north/south axis. In one society after another, northerners see themselves as economically vigorous, industrious, hardworking, reliable, serious, and thrifty, while southerners see themselves as socially refined, patient, obliging, amiable, and generous.[13]

Stories about the South tend to be stories about what it means to be modern. The South often appears as the locus of the non-modern (as in so much country music or *The Andy Griffith Show* or *The Waltons*) or of the modern world gone bad (as in *Deliverance* or Walker Percy novels). People have long projected onto the South their longing for a place free from the pressures of making a profit, free from loneliness and isolation; for just as long, others have projected onto the South their disgust (and maybe their own anxiety) with those unable or unwilling to keep up with the headlong rush into the future. The South is made to bear a lot of metaphorical baggage.[14]

The South has become an object of fun, a sanctioned way to laugh at poverty and backwardness in a way that has been banished for every other group. Pathetically, Southerners seem to have a habit of projecting ridicule onto the Southern state next to them, especially if it happens to be a bit poorer. So, for example, why can't they take a group photo of the people in _____ (insert your favorite object of ridicule here)? Because every time the photographer yells "cheese," all the people line up single file for a government handout. Or, what is the state flower of _____ (your least favorite Southern state here)? The satellite dish. Inbreeding seems to be an especially popular topic for these jokes, signifying the South's isolation and perversion born of being out of the mainstream of American life.

It is an interesting question to ask why these jokes are culturally sanctioned, why it is deemed permissible to make jokes about white Southerners that we can make about no one else. Partly, I think, it is because white Southerners are not "really" ethnic; they are not marked by physical features, name, or religion, the markers we recognize as authentic, as so powerful as to be above humor. Partly, it is because white Southerners seem to have brought on their own troubles, with their slavery, racism, and attachment to the past. Partly too it is because Southerners, ambivalent about their place in the nation, tell the jokes to inoculate themselves against the same jokes told against them. Like a member of a "true" ethnic group, a white Southerner is expected to be conscious of his or her regional identity—not fanatical but not indifferent. To be fanatical is to be sadly wedded to a lost cause; to ignore it is to be pretentious, to pretend to be something you are not. It is a fine line.[15]

Accent is the closest attribute white Southerners have to a physical marker to separate them from other white Americans; the same is true among blacks. These accents, which may seem a trivial, vestigial difference are in fact rich in meaning and consequence. Precisely because language seems, unlike physical attributes, to be at least partly under the control of its speaker, it is often taken as the key measure of national belonging. Accent accentuates difference where there is supposed to be commonality; it testifies to an inability or unwillingness to go along, to fit in. In the American case, accent is a marker of class and economic integration as well as regional identity. A Southern accent is often understood, inside the South as well as beyond its borders, as a symbol of poor education, low ambition, and reactionary politics.

Southern accents in fact offer a useful way to understand the evolution of the South. Despite the imagined organic connections between culture and environment, for example, in which it is assumed that Southerners, because of their hot and debilitating climate, speak more slowly than people from other places, they do not. They actually speak about the same number of words in a given time as other Americans; those in the hottest parts of the South do not talk more slowly than their up-country counterparts. The widespread notions that people in isolated pockets of the region such as mountains or islands speak some vestige of "pure" Elizabethan English are, as one linguist puts it, "pretty much complete exaggerations." Southern accents were first commented on only in the mid-nineteenth century; a Southern accent may have not developed until whites and blacks assimilated with each other over a broad enough area to forge a common way of speaking.[16] While vocabulary is converging in the South with the rest of the country, grammar and pronunciation do not seem to be. Young people, especially women, drawl as much as older ones. In fact, Southern speech is becoming more distinct in some ways: The younger a person is, regardless of education, the more likely he or she is to pronounce "hem" like "him" and "pen" like "pin." It appears, finally, that migrants from the North are more likely to adapt to Southern speech patterns than to set an example for their new neighbors to emulate. In all these ways, the image of a naturally adapted, artifactual, and disappearing South seems belied by careful study of current practices.

The almost habitual identification of Southern culture with certain traits tends quickly to stereotype, as certain subregions, subgeographies, classes, genders, or races become identified as carriers of certain characteristics. These traits in turn are given varying moral meanings, depending on the use to which they are put. Most of the debates over Southern culture over the generations have involved, for the most part, switching the moral value attached to a given trait. Thus plain folk, who were long seen as without ambition, are now seen as demonstrating a healthy aversion to the soulless capitalist market; former slaves whom previous generations of Northern and Southern whites saw as lazy were exercising their independence against white employers;

planters who many people in the nation thought were gracious and paternalistic were actually pretentious and patronizing. Many of the imagined traits, in other words, have remained the same; we merely change their meaning to suit our purposes.

We tend to tell the story of this distinct South from the relatively narrow point of view of our nation-state; we are provincial in our understanding of provinciality. The traditional, poor, and leisurely South takes on a different aspect when we step offshore, when we take a perspective not defined by the bounds of the nation-state. From the viewpoint of the Caribbean or much of South America or even parts of Europe the American South appears, throughout its history, as rich and money-driven. From the perspective of nineteenth-century Brazil, for example, the other great slave society of the hemisphere, the nineteenth-century South was a land of cities and towns, railroads and steamboats, white democracy and equality. From the perspective of people of African descent elsewhere in the world, the South appeared not only as a place of lynching and segregation but also as a place of relative black progress and possibility. Rather than The South, the Exception, the South becomes mostly American.[17]

But Americans seldom portray The South that way. Instead it is shown as the tropical corner of the nation, as the Latin America of North America. We rarely see movies or television shows set in the cold winters of Alabama or Texas, the ice storms of Georgia and Tennessee. Cotton bolls are always bursting white; heat rises in waves off the blacktop in a place where it seems always August. In fact, geography seems to many people a virtually inevitable reason for The South to take the shape it did, for the Civil War to tear the nation in two along a natural, almost perforated line. Despite generations of historians' work, many Americans still believe that the Civil War was the unavoidable result of an agrarian economy locked in battle with its natural adversary to the North, a sort of blameless struggle between the old and the new. The war seemed to await only the development of the North into an industrial economy sufficiently modern to resent and overpower its rural adversary. After passing through something like an adolescent crisis, the nation could get on with its destiny.

But did the North and South simply ripen into what they were destined to be all along? Few would have thought so in 1800, nearly two hundred years after the beginning of English and African arrival. It was only then, as the Industrial Revolution in Britain geared up, that the South became the Cotton South. The Southern landscape has proved itself remarkably adaptable ever since, the "natural" landscape for backwoods farmers, opulent planters, coal miners, discount store magnates, soybean farmers, and toxic waste dumpers. The South trails off into the North and the West in a disappointingly vague way, as it did in 1861 until last-minute votes, bloody guerrilla conflicts, and presidential maneuvering decided where the region ended for the time being.[18]

In fact, there was never a time when Southern culture developed secure from the outside, when people knew just where the borders were, when people knew just what the South was and was not. Southerners of every sort, from the eighteenth century to the present, lived at the intersection of many lines of influence. Power and prestige often came not merely as the result of knowing the right people locally, of marrying into the right neighborhood family. It was the white man who knew what was going on in the state capital and in Washington who had the most power, the man who had access to capital and information from New York or London who really made money; the political power and credit in turn allowed a man to hold office, to build a mansion, to become, ironically, stereotypically "Southern." Perhaps most tellingly, it was the men who went to West Point, who served the United States in its war with Mexico, who became identified as the prototypical white Southerners, Jefferson Davis and Robert E. Lee.[19]

From its very beginning, the white South saw itself as a particular strain of British culture, adapting parts of British identity that seemed to fit at the time. In the earliest days of the Chesapeake, military models provided the standard; as men and women began to establish farms to grow tobacco, the English yeomanry provided the script; as the farms grew into larger plantations worked by slaves, younger sons of the English gentry created an image of themselves as landed aristocrats. There was nothing dishonest or delusional about this; these white Southerners thought of themselves as colonial Englishmen. Just as other Englishmen abroad later wore pith helmets and operated mines, Southern Englishmen owned slaves and ran plantations. Southerners in fact did not so much emulate the North as borrow many of the same materials from England that the North borrowed. Sometimes, as with the cult of honor, the North borrowed something only to jettison it in a few decades, while the South held on for generations longer.

The black people of the South made their own adjustments, holding on to what they could of Africa, taking what they were forced to take or what they wanted to take of Britain. As genera-tions passed, a distinctly African American set of practices and styles developed and spread across the face of the South. Neither white nor black Southerners of course failed to see the differ-ences between themselves and those of other skin color. African Southerners reveled in their music, their crafts, their language, and their collective memories; European Southerners reveled in their literacy, their technology, and their political power. Yet many commonalities between black and white emerged, with influences running both directions, sometimes in obvious ways, sometimes almost imperceptibly. White and black, despite their hatred and mutual suspicion, found that their taste in food, in lan-guage, and in religion came to bear strong affinities.

Evangelicalism exemplifies the way nineteenth-century Southern culture developed. Evangelical religion became, over several decades, the great continuity and commonality in Southern culture. But it was not there at all at the beginning, when Englishmen from certain parts of the homeland supposedly brought the germ of Southern culture with them. Rather, heart religion was imported from England and took on a peculiarly Southern style because of the contribution of—and the problems presented by—African Americans. The importation of Baptists and Methodists came a full 150 years after Jamestown, but now it is religion that seems to set the South apart the most, that is the basis for much of its polit-ical conservatism, that earns it the label of Bible Belt, that seems to grow stronger rather than fade.

The South's most distinctive political feature, its stark biracial-ism, also constantly reflected changes in the larger Atlantic world.

The preferred mode of white dominion changed from that of a distant patriarch in the eighteenth century to a kind of paternalism in the Victorian era to a kind of managerial race relations in the late nineteenth and early twentieth centuries. In every instance, white Southerners followed the best ideals of European, especially English, dominion. They were not merely trying to please the metropole but were doing what they did in other facets of their lives, trying to make the best deal they could with the central ideas and tenets of the civilization of which they considered themselves a part while maintaining their divergent economic interests and their pride.

It was for this reason that white Southerners felt so wounded and outraged when they were charged with inhumanity as slaveholders. They claimed, with some justice, that they were doing nothing that Northerners and Englishmen had not done for generations, nothing that the Bible and the Constitution did not at least tacitly sanction. The rules seemed to change virtually overnight. The white South charged that it was the North that was changing, that was altering the rules. White Southerners, finding themselves on the defensive, quickly began to do something they had not done before, to assemble, entirely from materials available in the larger Anglo-American culture, a picture of themselves as a distinctive people with a separate history, culture, and destiny.

During the high tide of antebellum culture and sectionalism, in the 1850s, white Southern nationalists eagerly pored over the newspapers, journals, and books of Britain and Europe, finding there raw material with which to create a vision of the South as a misunderstood place. Sir Walter Scott, Lord Byron, Goethe, Italian and German nationalists, Karl Marx—they all helped create an image of people in search of their true identities, in conflict with the materialistic modern world. White Southern slaveholders did not merely find themselves different, naturally and organically, and then rebel as a result but rather created an idiom of exaggerated coherent uniqueness out of European ideals because they believed they had been rebelled against by their erstwhile countrymen. Slavery provided the impetus, but Britain, Europe, and the North supplied the language, the audience Southerners sought to appease, and the people against whom they defined themselves. The commonality as well as the difference fed the Civil War.[20]

The founders of the Confederacy saw themselves as participating in a widespread European movement, the self-determination of a people to be contained within its "natural" boundaries, boundaries that coincided with economic interests, with shared beliefs, with a way of life. As the Confederacy was born, people throughout the South recognized the need for all the paraphernalia of a nation and made it up on the spot. They used such modern means as contests advertised in newspapers and facsimiles of the founding Confederate documents suitable for framing. Southerners had paid close attention throughout the 1840s and 1850s to the strategies of European nationalists and were ready, even if, as Drew Faust has put it, "the emphasis placed by European nationalist thinkers on political differentiation based on separate race, language, religion, and history was problematic for white, English-speaking southerners." Like other nationalists in other places then and since, forced to make the most of trivial, even nonexistent cultural differences, white Southerners invested their nation with what they imagined to be a "racial" difference between the cold Anglo-Saxons of the North and their own heated Norman heritage. Confederates exhorted their countrymen to purge their language of Yankeeisms or Africanisms, to speak no "corrupt provincial dialect, but the noble undefiled English language." The Confederacy did not think of itself as something new, a dangerous experiment, but as the natural embodiment of something well established.[21]

We are accustomed now to conceive of the Confederacy as doomed from the beginning, but nations have been built of less sturdy economic and cultural materials. In fact, we are now beginning to see that as a recent study of nationalism has put it, "most nations have always been culturally and ethnically diverse, problematic, protean and artificial constructs that take shape very quickly and come apart just as fast." Even England, the first modern nation, found a common identity only in opposition to France. The defining war of the South came before the Southern nation was much more than an idea, before any deep or wide identity as Southerners—rather than as Virginians, Carolinians, or Texans, say—could develop.[22]

The Civil War was an extraordinarily unlikely event. While people long predicted some sort of conflict, few people, North or South, would have predicted anything like the war that occurred. Would the white South have fought for the right to expand slavery had it known that it would sacrifice a quarter of a million of its men in the process? Would the North have fought for the "mystic chords" of a unified nation had it had any idea of the cost in blood? Who could have known that the war would become a war to abolish slavery, immediately, without compensation to slaveholders?

The war could easily have turned out differently, with a different nation-state, with generations more of slavery, with an American apartheid. Yet we tend to talk of the South for generations beforehand as if it had known the toll it was going to extract from the nation; we equate the North with the Union for generations beforehand, as if New England had not threatened to leave the nation before Southerners considered such a move. In other words, Americans have grown far too comfortable with the Civil War, lulled into assuming its inevitability and its outcome, granting it a moral purpose it assumed only gradually and against the will of many who fought for the Union. We look back on the South's secession as a violation of the natural order, of the way things had to be, but one does not have to be a Dixiecrat to realize that the defeat of the Old South is often used to glorify the current nation-state, to sanctify America's destiny, to suggest the divine favor we enjoy, to show that through blood, we overcame the original sin of this country. It is too simple a story, both for the North and for the South.[23]

Many white Southerners have wanted to have it both ways: to be staunch Americans, proud of the nation-state, and to be true Southerners, unashamed of their forefathers' rebellion. They have not found it that hard to do. The process began early. As much as white Southerners believed in their right to secede, so the identities of Confederate and American proved to be surprisingly easy for most people to reconcile as soon as the war itself was over. A nationalism that had been constructed on the spot, imagined, could be easily dismantled. Even diehard Southerners could see their dual loyalties. An old Confederate who lived in Atlanta during Reconstruction taunted the Union soldiers on the street. "'You may have won the war,' he'd say, 'but we sure whipped your ass at Chickamauga.' The irate soldiers hauled him to their commander, who berated the old man and made him swear out a loyalty oath to the USA. The next day, the old man was back at his post on the street. When the Union soldiers walked by, he was ready. 'We may have won the war,' he yelled, 'but the Rebels sure whipped our ass at Chickamauga!'" This was an enforced convolution, of course, but white Southerners have willingly performed similar ideological gymnastics ever since Appomattox.[24]

The Confederate flag embodies the conflict. For some white Southerners, no other symbol seems as rich with meaning. When pressed to explain that meaning, some defenders speak in inarticulate and deeply felt terms of heritage, of great-great-grandfathers, of rights, of hypocritical Yankees, in language with no power to persuade anyone who does not already agree with them. When they speak of slavery, they speak of it only to deny that it had anything at all to do with the war, refusing to accept overwhelming evidence that runs counter to their beliefs. To the defenders of the battle flag, to be ashamed of the symbol is to be ashamed of who they are, of who their family has been. It seems a matter of all or nothing, of denying that history changes the meaning of things. To other defenders of the flag, the explicit connection to the past is not essential. They are not certain that they had ancestors who fought in the Civil War, yet they display the flag with even greater frequency and ardor than any Son of the Confederacy (indeed, to

the Sons' dismay) for the flag to them is a *rebel* flag. They are often
rebels with only a vague cause; the flag is such a multipurpose
symbol precisely because it is so vague. It is a sign of resistance to
the boss, to Southern yuppies, to the North, to blacks, to liberals,
to any kind of political correctness. In their eyes, the rebel flag
stands for the same thing that they imagine it stood for in 1861:
Leave Me the Hell Alone.

The Confederate flag is a topic of such debate and divisiveness
in the South today because it denies all that black and white
Southerners shared, because it reduces the South to a one-time
and one-sided political identity. The South and the Confederacy
covered the same territory, shared a critical part of history, but
they have never been synonymous—not even between 1861 and
1865. Confederate symbolism has spread to places that were
staunchly Unionist in the Civil War itself; drive through the
mountain counties of the South, even West Virginia, and notice
how many Confederate flags you see, how many people imagine a
connection with the Confederacy they have no genealogical or
geographical right to claim, how many people seize on what is
supposedly a discredited symbol of an aborted nationalism. The
Confederacy lives on as a potent symbol, its potency coming from
its ambiguity and instability of meaning, a meaning that was not
unambiguous even in 1861.

That same ambiguity has permitted white Northerners to use
the Civil War for another purpose, dubious and simplistic in its
own way. Many of them have tended to see themselves ever since
the war as the chosen, the redeemed, the real nation; black freedom seems a good not only for its own sake but as an emblem of a

larger national destiny and freedom. This role has served to sanctify the North and the West and to make the South a sink of iniquity, a focus and explanation for what is lacking in the country in general. The Civil War seems to many white non-Southerners to absolve their ancestors from complicity in slavery for the 250 years before Appomattox. It is this willful forgetfulness that gives credence to charges of Northern hypocrisy from diehard defenders of the Confederacy, who insist that slavery was a national crime and not a purely sectional one.

Southern novelists such as William Faulkner have looked the convoluted Southern mythology in the face, trying to see what it might mean (and, ironically, giving it worldwide attention and credence). "Don't you see?" Faulkner's Ike McCaslin yells at a black man in "The Bear." "This whole land, the whole South, is cursed, and all of us who derive from it whom it ever suckled, white and black both, lie under the curse?. . . . What corner of Canaan is this?" [25]

A corner of Canaan: That may be as good a description of the South as we are going to get. At its very heart, the South has been, and is, a problematic province of Canaan, the land of milk and honey. White Southerners have shared in the national sense of the United States as a peculiarly bountiful, democratic, and idealistic nation but have always understood that they are not quite as bountiful, democratic, or idealistic as their countrymen in other parts of the nation. It is that tension that underlies the centuries-old struggle to explain the South.

Space, along with time, forms the unavoidable contexts in which we live our lives. People *will* think spatially and historically. But we can be more self-conscious about the *way* we think in these dimensions. The categories in which we place things have everything to do with what we take those things to be. Better, it seems, to talk first of concrete things—poverty and power, specific people with specific interests—rather than of a gaseous Southern "culture" or a suspiciously malleable and sanitized "heritage." We need to see the many connections between local and state, local and national, local and international. We need to recognize the structures of economy, ideology, religion, fashion, and politics that cut across the South, connecting some individuals with allies and counterparts elsewhere. We need to see both how permeable the boundary between North and South has always been and how regional difference is constantly being reinvented across that boundary. We need to recognize how willingly most white people outside the South supported slavery and segregation, how the movement to end Jim Crow grew up among black Southerners before it was impressed as a problem on the rest of the nation.

Southern history is made up of the things that have happened and are happening on this artificially bounded piece of real estate, however contradictory they may have been and remain. Southern history bespeaks a place that is more complicated than the stories we tell about it. Throughout its history the South has been a place where poverty and plenty have been thrown together in especially jarring ways, where democracy and oppression, white and black, slavery and freedom, have warred. The very story of the South is a story of unresolved identity, unsettled and restless, unsure and defensive. The South, contrary to so many words written in defense and in attack, was not a fixed, known, and unified place, but rather a place of constant movement, struggle, and negotiation.[26]

There is a tendency for Southerners to see time as the enemy, erasing the inscriptions on the land, destroying whatever certain identity the South has ever had. Louis Rubin, a leading commentator on Southern literature, returned to his birthplace of Charleston, South Carolina, only to find the signs of his childhood gone. "On each successive visit to what had once been my home, I found that what had constituted its substance and accidence both had dwindled." He felt that his childhood and his Southern identity were "becoming more and more a matter of absence, loss, and alienation. I was, that is, steadily becoming dispossessed." But Rubin, recognizing the self-centeredness, the selfishness, of such a view, chose to redefine his relation to the South and the changes both he and the region have undergone, seeking "identity in time, not outside it. Its diminution did not represent merely loss, but change, of which I was a part, and which, because it had happened to me in my time, was mine to cherish, . . . proof that I had been and still was alive."[27]

Those people, black and white, who care about their particular South should take heart from a vision in which regional identity is constantly being replenished, even as other forms, older forms, erode and mutate. Anything that has happened and is happening in this corner of the country rightfully belongs to the South's past, whether or not it seems to fit the template of an imagined Southern culture. There is no essence to be denied, no central theme to violate, no role in the national drama to be betrayed. The South is continually coming into being, continually being remade, continually struggling with its pasts.

A DIGITAL CIVIL WAR

I HAD AN idea for a book in September 1991: "I will tell the story of two communities, one Northern and one Southern, across the era of the Civil War. I hope to write a relatively brief book that students in the United States survey or general readers can turn to for a compelling account of the difference the Civil War made in the lives of people on both sides of the conflict." After the lengthy book I had just completed, a history of the South from Reconstruction into the early twentieth century, I longed for history "on a human scale, examining life before, during, and after the events of the battlefield, relating the story of blacks as well as whites, women as well as men, defeat as well as victory."

For a historian, there had never been a time like the Civil War, a time when people of every sort documented their lives in such detail in letters, diaries, and memoirs. There had never been a time when the government kept such careful records in the census and the military. I knew from speaking and teaching that many people longed to understand the Civil War more clearly and fully. I included myself in that number, for I was by no means an expert on the war. I had slowly come to feel its pull and its centrality in Americans' conception of themselves, but I had much to learn.

I had some notion of what I wanted to do. I wanted to deal with both the North and the South in a comparative story. I wanted to understand two places close to the border between the North and the South to see how people in such proximity and similarity could go to war. I wanted to integrate military history and social history. I wanted to try my hand at a kind of social history in which I followed characters throughout a story. I did not have a particular thesis to push. The form of the story—two intertwined community histories—was the compelling thing to me at the outset.

I needed good records to accomplish such a book. So I sat down with maps and guides to military units and indexes of newspapers to find two counties centrally involved in the Civil War start to finish. It did not take long to see that two places stood out: Augusta County, Virginia, and Franklin County, Pennsylvania. Lying about two hundred miles apart in the Great Valley that cuts across the Mason-Dixon Line, these two communities were similar in many ways. The ethnic backgrounds of the white population, the climate, soil, and crops, the religious denominations and political parties of the two places shared a great deal.

Only one real difference divided the two places: slavery. Five thousand enslaved people, about a fifth of the population, lived in Augusta. As I wrote in my proposal, slavery had become woven "into the economy, the political beliefs, and the hearts of white residents of the Valley." Although many of the Virginians in the

Valley "harbored doubts, public and private, about the Confederate cause and its effects on Virginia, most threw themselves into the fight once the line had been drawn." The situation in Pennsylvania "bore its own ambiguities and tensions. White Pennsylvanians, after all, did not hesitate to circumscribe black rights and opportunities; in the districts so close to the Mason-Dixon Line sympathizers with the South were more visible than abolitionists. Yet white Pennsylvanians fought and died in a war that became a war to end slavery, finding ideals and aspirations they had not held before."

It was the sudden and powerful redefinition of people on both sides that drove my imagination. I could understand how Massachusetts and South Carolina had grown to hate each other, but New England and the deep South did not fight the Civil War alone. It required the recruitment of the border South into the Confederacy and the border North into the Union cause to create the continent-wide struggle that the Civil War became. An irony was obvious: The border would be the battlefield for a war that white people on the border resisted until the last moment. And no place played a more critical role as a corridor for invading armies of both sides than the Great Valley. One of the richest, most favored, and most Unionist places in the nation became one of the places most ravaged by the war.

Almost immediately the title of the project came to me: the Valley of the Shadow. I wanted to strike a note of gravity in this study of the Civil War, to remind ourselves that war was about death as much as it was about anything else. The biblical words seemed fitting, since Christianity served as the common foundation of the North and the South.

Most of the themes I explored for the next twelve years were there at the beginning. The one thing I did not mention in the four-and-a-half-page sketch was computers. Yet within six months I completely recast my understanding of the project so that it could no longer be imagined without these machines.

Like others of my generation, I grew up with an image of computers as massive, alien things far removed from my life other than as the generator of phone bills. But when I arrived at graduate school in 1975, I discovered that to do history of the sort I wanted to do, I had to learn about computing and statistics. There seemed no other way to understand the experiences of people who left few written records of their own, the patterns of whose lives had to be pieced together from fragments. Over the preceding decade the "new social history" had been transforming the profession. One book after another reshaped our understanding of social mobility, community, demography, economics, family life, and slavery. New kinds of classes appeared in the graduate offerings, and new kinds of faculty were hired.

I caught the fever. When I decided to focus on a history of crime and punishment in the American South in the nineteenth century, it seemed to me that any study of crime had to try to count offenses and offenders, though crime is notoriously difficult to measure even in the present. I quizzed my mother, a veteran of the mimeograph machine, on how to cut a stencil for a form on which I could record all the crimes in three Georgia counties across the nineteenth century. I then camped out in front of a microfilm reader in Atlanta in 1978 and coded crimes from handwritten court records for weeks on end, all in the faith that some interesting patterns would emerge from the data after I fed them into the computer back in New Haven.

There were only two problems: I did not know how to use the computer or how to do statistics. I taught myself the rudiments of the latter with a textbook and some videotapes. I taught myself the former by trial and error, especially error. Eventually I figured out the machinery enough to get some reasonable-looking numbers for a dissertation. I made some tables and graphs that I could not have made without the computer, and they held some surprises that shaped my dissertation and thus my first book. The computer had proved to be a useful, if sometimes reluctant, ally.

In 1985, thanks to the beneficence of the University of Virginia, I got my very own personal computer on which to do research for my history of the New South. It boasted a color monitor, a hard drive able to hold 10 megabytes, and a 2400-baud external modem. Trying to live up to such a machine, I learned to use yet another mainframe computer interactively, punch cards having been thrown on the computing trash heap. I taught myself multiple regression analysis and other things contrary to my character and abilities. But the real excitement came in the discovery of electronic mail. The combination of written language, informality, and efficiency—and, in the mid-1980s, the feeling of being among the information technology elite—proved surprisingly satisfying.

I enjoyed that feeling of seeing the future in e-mail and list serves, but in the early 1990s I saw such machinery as only an accessory of my professional life. I struggled to generate the tables that lay at the back of my book manuscript on the New South. I invested vast energy and consumed considerable self-esteem in producing what turned out to be quite unattractive maps. I swore I would never attach my work so closely to the fickle, expensive, and cold machinery of computing. In fact, I thought up the Valley of the Shadow book as an antidote to the computer. The new book would be handmade of native materials, crafted in quiet and solitary hours in the archives.

My plan failed. Trying to achieve a token balance on the committee that oversaw computing at my university, someone appointed me to a committee dominated by scientists, physicians, and engineers. I had long been underfoot in the Engineering School's computer labs, consuming valuable time in front of UNIX workstations. I had become known to the programmers and administrators of the Academic Computing office through my incessant questions. I went to the committee meetings in the fall of 1991 with some trepidation.

At one of the first meetings we learned that IBM was interested in helping computing at the university and wanted our committee to suggest a joint venture. We batted ideas around for a while. I timorously noted that many of us in the humanities had no computers on our desks; maybe we could do something with English or History, well-respected departments at the University of Virginia. There was some good-natured joshing among the electrical engineers and medical imaging specialists about aiding the third world of computing over in the humanities, but what could we do for such backward people who showed so little interest in helping themselves? Virtually all my humanist colleagues, it was true, seemed content with what little computing was provided us. No clamor of discontent arose from the offices where type-writers banged out their familiar QWERTY rhythms.

But the chairman of the committee, William Wulf, saw, to my surprise, some possibility in my self-interested suggestion. Wulf, a pioneer in the creation of the Internet (and, I learned later, the proud father of a young historian), argued that if we could connect the talents in UVa's excellent humanities departments with farsighted computer scientists and robust computers, we might be on to something. What if we really could use computers to help make sense of the great store of human knowledge and striving locked away in archives and books? What if computers were just getting good enough for humanists to use, now that they could deal with images as easily as they could with numbers, now that computers were networked and had enough storage space to hold the vast and messy stuff historians habitually collected?

Bill Wulf asked if I knew of any likely humanists who might be willing to consider experimenting with such an enterprise. I had to admit that I did not. He asked me what I was working on. I smiled and told him about my brand-new, computer-free idea for a book on the Civil War. I was happy to serve on his committee to help repay my friends in computing for all their help with my last book—currently in press—but really, I had no intention of taking on a new engagement with computers.

But as I described the Civil War book, with its close attention to millions of details, its determination to find patterns hidden in masses of scattered records, I realized that it would be perfect for computers. I was describing a large database project with many variables drawn from diverse sources. From that step I made a short leap to my teaching experience. For years I had required that my students read, on microfilm, a year of a newspaper from any place in the South and write an essay on the most striking thing they found in its pages. Later I sent them into Special Collections in our library, throwing them into dozens of collections of letters, diaries, and account books, telling them to find out what it was like to own people or to be considered property. There was nothing like confronting the raw material of the past to understand history and to feel its powerful appeal.

When I combined the idea of putting all the material necessary for my book in a large database with the idea of allowing other people access to that same material, I had the basic idea for the Valley of the Shadow Project. Bill Wulf and Alan Batson, a seasoned computer scientist and head of Academic Computing, knew what we had to do: combine humanists with programmers of breadth and flexibility so that they could work together as a team. I readily agreed, for I had no intention of learning, and no ability to learn, all the things I would require to do such a project on my own.

We also knew we needed other humanists. Fortunately, one of the best-known members of the faculty at UVa long had an interest in the representation of texts. Jerome McGann of our English department quickly joined the core team. Unlike me, McGann had in mind a project that was perfectly suited for computing, the collected works of Dante Gabriel Rossetti, the pre-Raphaelite English painter and poet who intertwined his works across time, subject, and media. McGann, famous as the editor of the works of Byron and a pioneer in historically grounded editing, was far ahead of me in the theory of such work. Fortunately, we quickly became friends and allies despite the obvious disparity of our subjects—luminous paintings of haunting women, for his part, and prosaic census records and battle maps, for mine.

With our founding premise, two projects, and a name, the Institute for Advanced Technology in the Humanities (IATH), we did a demo for IBM.[1] We created a series of images, scanned and linked to a numeric keypad. The images were of a census page, a newspaper page, a letter, a period map of a neighborhood of the Northern community, and a computer-generated topographical map of the Southern county. "Imagine," I told the visitors from IBM, "that we create a powerful database to unite all these diverse kinds of media so that people can be their own historians. Users will be able to find their own patterns in the data, draw their own conclusions based on evidence. Think of it as a research library in a box, enabling students at places without a large archive to do the same kind of research as a professional historian." At this point I assumed that we would record the data on a tape and then make it available to other institutions that had the machinery to run it. I could not imagine making the data available over the Internet, and no one else did either.

To our gratification, IBM agreed to donate a number of power-ful workstations, a server, and a technical adviser. The work-stations boasted one-gigabyte hard drives and seventeen-inch high-resolution monitors and ran UNIX. They worked in concert with a strong server that permitted far greater manipulations of images and databases than any personal computer could. We also purchased a tape drive that allowed us to store the enormous files we began to create. Just as important, the library gave us space, one of the most valued commodities in a university, to build the institute. Symbolically the library moved the microfilm over which my students and I had labored for so many hours to make space for this new kind of scholarship. The library had just created its own Electronic Text Center, dedicated to putting texts in machine-readable form.

Thanks to our alliance with the library, we soon learned about something called SGML (Standard Generalized Markup Language). Although we joked that the letters stood for "sounds good, maybe later," we quickly came to see its power. The idea of SGML, which had been developing for years within the library community, was to annotate, or "tag," text so that computers would recognize the functional role of the text. Thus a search for the name Brown would return a valid search only when those letters spelled someone's name, not a color. This technique meant that textual searches could gain some of the precision and clarity of numerical searches.

As promising as SGML and other techniques might be, they left unresolved the single largest problem for the humanities, getting material into the computer in the first place. We paid to have a company automatically scan and digitize about ten thousand pages of newspapers from microfilm, but there was no software that would conveniently handle such images, so we had to rely on awkward file formats and image-manipulation tools. Those newspaper pages, set in type seven generations earlier, had then been subjected to wars, water, fungus, neglect, tape, and sometimes careless microfilming. Even more challenging, much of the other evidence in the Valley Project was handwritten. Not only had letters and diaries been produced in pen and ink, but so had tens of thousands of names in the population, agricultural, manufacturing, and slaveholder censuses. My original dreams of the automatic conversion of text by optical character recognition died a quick, if painful, death. There would be no choice but to transcribe nearly everything that went into the digital archive. And so we began the seemingly endless task with a few hours of labor by work-study graduate students.

Slowly the digital archive began to take shape. We amassed enough transcribed newspaper articles, names from the census, diaries and letters, and military records to create prototypes of the databases of those records. We scanned enough maps and images to show what those would look like in the archives.

I began to explore the world of hypertext, about which I had been completely unaware before I plunged into the Valley Project. It turned out to have a fascinating history and a direct connection to the practice of history.

Vannevar Bush had served as the director of the Office of Scientific Research and Development throughout World War II. At war's end Bush sought an uplifting purpose for the nation's scientists. New tools had recently appeared, the *Atlantic Monthly* explained in its introduction to an article Bush published in 1945, that promised to "give man access to and command over the inherited knowledge of the ages." The essay, "As We May Think," used the writing of history to suggest the possibilities of the future. Bush saw great promise in photography and microfilm, and he foresaw the role of the copying machine and the fax as well as the revolution in numerical computing. But he reserved his excitement for something broader than any specific machinery.

The human mind, Bush observed, "operates by association. With one item in its grasp, it snaps instantly to the next that is suggested by the association of thoughts, in accordance with some intricate web of trails carried by the cells of the brain." Bush marveled that "the speed of action, the intricacy of trails, the detail of mental pictures, is awe-inspiring beyond all else in nature." He wondered if one could make a machine that worked that way, that could remember the evanescent trails and weave them into lasting patterns. He described a machine he called the memex, a wonderful imaginary device of glass, steel, and microfilm, levers, screens, and reels. Bush turned to history to suggest why we needed such a thing:

> The owner of the memex, let us say, is interested in the origin and properties of the bow and arrow. Specifically he is studying why the short Turkish bow was apparently superior to the English long bow in the skirmishes of the Crusades. He has dozens of possibly pertinent books and articles in his memex. First he runs through an encyclopedia, finds an interesting but sketchy article, leaves it projected. Next, in a history, he finds another pertinent item, and ties the two together. Thus he goes, building a trail of many items. Occasionally he inserts a comment of his own, either linking it into the main trail or joining it by a side trail to a particular item. When it becomes evident that the elastic properties of available materials had a great deal to do with the bow, he branches off on a side trail which takes him through textbooks on elasticity and tables of physical constants. He inserts a page of longhand analysis

of his own. Thus he builds a trail of his interest through the maze
of materials available to him.

This fascinating vision never came to pass in this mechanical and
photographic form, but the basic idea behind it, an associative,
multilinear way of representing information, lived on.

Ted Nelson, an eccentric visionary, developed the idea of electronic hypertext in the 1960s and 1970s but was unable to build a
workable model. HyperCard, a program that ran on Apple computers, allowed linking of discrete cards in "stacks" in a rudimen-
tary form of hypertext. In the 1980s the Intermedia team at
Brown University, under the leadership of George Landow, created elegant hypertextual projects such as The Dickens Web and
The *In Memoriam* Web, also running on Apple computers. Their
work held some of the same aspirations as ours—the linkage of
disparate but related materials to create rich contexts for teaching
and research in the humanities—and they had built superb examples of hypertext with documents, maps, illustrations, and time-
lines. But at the time we conceived IATH, Intermedia had
recently disbanded because of its loss of funding and its reliance
on proprietary software. In 1992 Mark Bernstein of Eastgate
Systems too released Storyspace, a sophisticated hypertext tool in
which experimental novels were already being written. But as
appealing as it was, Storyspace was a stand-alone and proprietary
tool, not the networked model we were struggling toward.[2]

In my own discipline of history, a team of talented scholars was
producing an electronic version of their textbook, *Who Built
America?* Hearing of their effort from a colleague, I visited Roy

Rosenzweig at his home outside Washington in the fall of 1992. Rosenzweig showed me a version of his team's beautiful work, which they were producing as part of a series of electronic projects published by a company called Voyager. Unlike the Valley Project, the *Who Built America?* disk, designed for Apple computers, boasted film clips, sound, and elegant visual design, all wrapped around a narrative history of the United States in the Gilded Age. It also had considerable funding and a distribution network, neither of which we possessed. Rosenzweig was generous with his time, knowledge, and contacts. I was glad to see another historian engaged in the digital enterprise but a bit disheartened. Their project, covering all U.S. history for the half century after the Civil War, made commercial and pedagogical sense in a way that my much more narrowly focused study did not. *Who Built America?* was officially released a year later.

We were going down a different road, using UNIX, SGML, and other nonproprietary standards. This decision was not as obvious as it sounds in retrospect. The tools available to us at the beginning of the 1990s were powerful but crude. We could have produced quicker and more attractive versions of our projects if we had used proprietary software. But these tools, attractive in the short run, my colleagues in the library and computer science worlds persuaded me, would limit the ultimate result of our efforts.

The press proved to be interested in what *Computerworld* called in early 1993 "Technohumanities 101." Interviewed for the piece, I awkwardly described the electronic text I had in mind: "You come to a footnote and you click on it. Instead of getting the name of the newspaper from which I had drawn a quote, you can see the entire paper. Or you could click on a person and see where he lived on a beautiful color map." The journalist claimed that "the power of computers applied to newly digitized texts is literally turning into one-day undergraduate exercises what previously might have been the basis for a doctoral dissertation."[3] The *Christian Science Monitor* did a story a few weeks later and described the network at UVa in utopian terms: "One day every student will be able to reach any professor or retrieve any text from the university library."[4]

Such rhetoric was outrunning our actual accomplishment, for we had only the most fragmentary of sources in the project. Fortunately, in the summer of 1993 Anne Rubin, a graduate student who had arrived at UVa after her studies at Princeton, came on board. She spent the summer "marking up" the newspapers in SGML on the IBM workstation in my history office. (In homage to the historian C. Vann Woodward, I named the machine vann.) Anne worked from the scanned microfilm images, excerpting, summarizing, and transcribing articles so they would be searchable on the machine. By the fall we had enough articles on-line to show the possibilities of searching for names, subjects, and dates. We had also gathered enough of the population census and enough individual military records, kindly made available to us by the authors of two books on relevant units, to show how users of the project could weave together disparate sources to see patterns they could not see otherwise. We had built, in other words, a proof of concept. Only those of us working on the project realized just what a thin sliver of evidence we had yet prepared, what mountains of work loomed before us.

One day in the fall of 1993 Thorny Staples, associate director of IATH and responsible for building our earliest prototypes, e-mailed to say that I should come to his office as soon as I could. There he showed me Mosaic, a new tool for something its creator called the World Wide Web. The brainchild of an English physicist working in Switzerland, Mosaic had been designed for scientific collaboration. The Web, an overlay of linked text and image that used the Internet for its vehicle, redefined the experience of being on-line.

It was immediately apparent that everything had changed for our digital projects. Now we could see much more easily how to construct an archive online; our material—images, databases, and all—need not wait for years to be disseminated but could be shared even as we gathered it. The archive could reach anywhere in the world people could tie into the Internet, a network expanding exponentially. And to our great good fortune, the World Wide Web was built around something its creator called HTML, hypertext markup language, a subset of the SGML we had already adopted as the basic structure of our work at IATH. We would be able to build a site, as it was called, for this new web with relative ease.

The first Web version of the Valley Project appeared as a research report on the IATH Web site in 1993. It was not pretty: long stretches of text with a few grainy images and large red ball icons and numbers in blue and brackets for hyperlinks. Despite the unprepossessing appearance, my report made ambitious pronouncements. This electronic archive would not be "fully processed, exhausted by the imagination of the people who put it together. There is far more in the newspapers, censuses, military records, and the rest than we can contain in one narrative, far more connections than we could possibly hardwire in."We hoped that readers "will be tempted to construct their own narratives, connecting things we have not thought to connect, coming up with ideas that eluded us, adding to the ongoing construction of this history." Participation, action, and exploration—those were the hallmarks of the Valley Project. [5]

I needed money if we were to live up to these hopeful, even boastful words. It had become clear that the labor needs of the Valley Project would be enormous. I was determined that every student who worked on the project would be paid at a fair rate. We were innovating in the organization of humanities scholarship, and I wanted to make sure that we did not build this new work on an exploitative basis. The university had provided us with some start-up money, but we were quickly exhausting that. I had no commercial prospects for the Valley Project.

Fortunately, we found a partner in the Woodrow Wilson Birthplace and Museum. Wilson had been born in Staunton, the county seat of the Southern community in the Valley Project, in 1857, when his father served as minister of the First Presbyterian Church. The house, beautifully preserved, was dedicated to evoking the world of late-antebellum Staunton. The sophisticated staff at the birthplace saw possibilities in the Valley Project for enriching the understanding of its visitors. Staff members envisioned a terminal in the museum that would allow them and visitors the opportunity to explore daily life in the town. The birthplace and museum secured a grant of six thousand dollars from the Virginia Foundation for the Humanities so that we could continue building the project; we in turn happily agreed to set up a workstation there running the Valley Project. There was no way to hook to the Internet, so we configured the machine to run Mosaic from its hard drive.

The Augusta Archive, built from the outset for the World Wide Web, was the true prototype of the Valley Project. Unlike the linear and wordy research report, the archive put primary materials at center stage. Designed for use in a public place where we could not assume that visitors had ever used a computer before, much less the new World Wide Web, we supplied detailed directions and even provided the opportunity for people to click on a narration button to hear me assure them that "by using the mouse to point and click, you simply move through the screens that appear before you. There is much more in the archive than you can see in one visit. Just follow your intuition and interests." We tried to explain what to expect: "A search in the Augusta Archive is more like a scavenger hunt than finding an entry in an encyclopedia or playing a video game. Although the computing equipment is sophisticated, the records around which the archive is built were very much the product of the mid-nineteenth century." In other words, people should expect dead ends, misspellings, and blank spots not only because of the physical limitations of the records but also because of the bias of the propertied white men who created the documents in the first place.[6]

As we prepared to debut the Augusta Archive in the fall, we put on a big push in the summer of 1994. Anne Rubin oversaw six other students who joined us. We refined the search tools and learned how to make more attractive images. We finished the

1860 census and tagged newspapers through the late 1850s. We added a transcription of the registry of free blacks in Staunton and found a few diaries and letters in UVa's library. We made maps of the neighborhoods and connected images of historic houses to a painting of Staunton in 1857. The site began to look more coherent as we learned how to work on the Web.

Still, I longed for more firsthand testimony of the sort I had imagined three years earlier for the Valley of the Shadow book. The census and the newspaper were fine, but they did not speak to people the way I hoped. I wanted to find materials no one had seen before, diaries and letters locked away in family collections. Our friends at the Wilson birthplace in Staunton eagerly agreed to cosponsor what we called a History Harvest in the fall of 1994. We would show the Augusta Archive, newly installed in the museum, at the same time we tried to locate more compelling, more personal evidence.

The Charlottesville paper announced the event with a hopeful article: "In the dark, musty attics of Augusta County could lie never-before-told snippets of life during the Civil War. At least that's what University of Virginia historian Ed Ayers hopes to find when he shows up in Staunton this weekend, computer and high-tech scanner in hand."[7] We set up shop at the Wilson birthplace and waited. And we got some useful materials, a diploma from a local girls' school and a poster about deserters from the Confederacy. The most memorable moment for me came when A. R. Ware, Jr., a dapper elderly African American man, sat down at a computer for the first time. As we searched the free black registry, he pointed to one name after another that he knew. The interest he expressed in the project was what we all dreamed of. [8]

By this time the World Wide Web was spreading rapidly, giving us new audiences every day but ironically limiting what we could do. HTML proved a very tenuous mechanism for holding things together. In many ways, HTML set hypertext back from where it had been five years earlier, for it restricted flexibility and complexity in a way SGML did not. Worse, the limits of bandwidth faced by those who viewed the Web on modems—pretty much everyone except those in universities and corporations at that time—meant that we could not use images effectively. Many minutes passed while our newspaper images, maps, or photographs slowly filled in screens.

That was why that even as the Web grew in the mid-1990s, so did other forms of digital media, especially CD-ROMs. CDs held out a number of attractive possibilities for the Valley Project, allowing us to create a truly multimedia environment with rich color photographs, music, voice, and animations. Moreover, teachers told us they preferred CDs to the Web because it had already become clogged with pornography and other material they could not risk in their classrooms. The authoring environments for CDs were vastly more flexible than for the Web, and I dreamed of building something attractive and evocative as well as useful.

When Steve Forman, history editor at W. W. Norton & Company, approached me about publishing my forthcoming book on the Civil War, I made him a counteroffer. I would love to publish with Norton, I said, but before I could write a book, I had to build the Valley archive. Norton, like other publishers at the time, was interested in new media, and it had enjoyed some successes in the field. Would it be interested in working with us to produce a CD-ROM of the Valley of the Shadow? It turned out that it was, and we launched an effort to build a CD at the same time we were building the Web site. The raw material of the two would be the same, but the CD would present the data and lists and articles in an elegant format that would attract people far more than the unadorned Web. It was becoming clear that I would have to find a stream of funding if we were going to make it all the way through the Civil War, much less into Reconstruction. A sizable grant from the National Endowment for the Humanities arrived just in time to sustain the project for the next three years.

As people discovered the World Wide Web in the late 1990s, many discovered the Valley of the Shadow Project. What they found there was still very much a work in progress; we had a long way to go to complete the ambitious plans laid out in 1993. I wondered if I would ever meet those goals, especially when Anne Rubin, my crucial ally in the first years of the project, left, with my blessing, to finish her dissertation. Happily, I found a new ally.

William G. Thomas III had used the Valley of the Shadow while teaching at a school in Pennsylvania. Like other early adopters, Will quickly discovered limitations in our digital archive. The huge newspaper images took forever to load over the slow connections then available to most people, and he called me to suggest some improvements. A former doctoral student and a good friend, Will knew he could make such recommendations without offense.

As it turned out, Will moved to Charlottesville the following year and became project director for the Valley Project. We were just beginning work in earnest on the CD-ROM for Norton. A group of excellent professional musicians recorded original music at bargain rates. We produced three-dimensional models of Augusta and Franklin so that people could see the lay of the land. We linked census records with local maps, creating the kinds of tools the Web could not handle well. The CD-ROM, published in 2000 after enormous labors, received good reviews and won major prizes even though by that time the Web had stolen the spotlight from fixed media such as CDs. [9]

In the meantime, the Web site continued to develop. We kept finding material, especially once we got into the Civil War years. Will led teams of graduate and undergraduate students to transcribe thousands of compiled service records at the National Archives, to scan hundreds of photographs at the United States Army Military Institute library in Carlisle, Pennsylvania, and to locate diaries and letters in Franklin, in Augusta, and in libraries all over the country. People wrote us about sources they were eager to share from their family collections.

Will and Michael Mullins, a visiting graduate student from Australia, suggested that we use a floor plan as a way to convey the sense that visitors were working within different "rooms" as they worked with different sources. With a black-and-white octagonal image, a floor plan by Thomas Jefferson, we provided an overview of the entire archive. The octagon immediately became the most visible symbol of the Valley Project. Will turned the Virginia Center for Digital History, originally built around the Valley Project in 1998, into an incubator for a whole series of innovative sites on everything from Jamestown to the civil rights struggle.

Though I was by this time deep into writing the book based on the Valley Project, I continued to dream of a possibility I had glimpsed at the beginning of the enterprise almost a decade earlier, history in hypertext. The Valley Project was itself only an archive. Might there be a way to use the electronic environment to create forms of narrative or argument that took fuller advantage of the materials we had gathered?

At one of the many conferences devoted to the future of digital scholarship held in the late 1990s and early 2000s, participants worried if the academy would ever acknowledge the contributions of digital scholars, especially with the tangible rewards of tenure and promotion. Digital scholarship, after all, was something new and did not always fit into established disciplinary standards and practices. I warned that we should not expect history departments to acknowledge digital scholarship until it assumed the form that people recognized as real scholarship, scholarly argument in the form of a professional journal article or monograph. The editor of the *American Historical Review*, Michael Grossberg, attending the conference and interested in the possibilities of the new media, asked if I might be willing to undertake such a digital article based on the Valley Project. I told Michael that I would check with Will Thomas, and if he was game, I would be too. Will, typically, loved a challenge, and we plunged into the enterprise. Will had more at stake than I did, for the history department at Virginia would be considering him for tenure in two years.

Will and I could not address all the many issues the Valley Project made it possible to explore, so we focused on a key question for which most of the evidence had already been gathered: How different was the antebellum South from the antebellum North on the eve of the Civil War? We hoped that by measuring as precisely as possible the various facets of life in Franklin County and Augusta County—demography, land use, agriculture, industry, literacy, religion, gender, and race relations, among others— we could come up with a clearer answer to a question that had generated enormous discussion for many decades. Since Franklin and Augusta were alike in so many ways, from soil and climate to religion and white ethnicity, we thought that perhaps we could triangulate the role of slavery in a new way. We began to sift the evidence more finely than ever before, constructing elaborate geographic databases, detailed tables, and revealing quotations. We compiled bibliographies of the key writing on the issues.

We struggled to imagine how we might possibly contain and convey so much information. We knew that we did not want to use the computer merely as a distribution device; we wanted to rethink the ways that text could be presented on computer screens. That meant that we would need to write in discrete modules of prose, each module making one point clearly and connecting directly to the relevant evidence and relevant scholarly literature. Working with Kimberly Tryka, the associate director of the Virginia Center for Digital History, we began to construct various models. We used Extensible Markup Language (XML), which permitted us to make multiple dynamic links from each module.

We had to reinvent the most basic elements of scholarship. There could be no fixed page numbers, for example, since in a digital article people could start from many different places and follow many different paths. There would be no traditional foot-notes or an index. In other words, we were devising an argument for a journal article at the same time that we were envisioning the very form of a new kind of journal article. Could our colleagues be persuaded this was a worthwhile activity? Fortunately, the single most important criterion for historians is a plausible fit between evidence and argument. Since the digital archive we had already built emphasized evidence, our fellow historians could see that we were working within the empirical tradition of the profession even if we experimented with presentation. Will and I were by no means enemies of traditional forms; we both had written monographs and scholarly articles and planned to write more. We also avoided the language of obfuscation and disorientation that some theorists of literary hypertext had adopted.[10]

By the time we began our article in 2000, historians had already adapted to some aspects of the electronic environment. The president of the American Historical Association at the time, Robert Darnton, issued a call for using digital media: "Anyone who has done long stints of original research knows the feeling: If only my reader could have a look inside this dossier, at all the letters in it, not just the lines from the letter I am quoting. If only I could pursue that trail through the archives, despite the detour from my central argument. If only I could show how themes interweave through diverse bodies of documents, even though the patterns extend beyond the bounds of my narrative."

To bring that feeling into reality, Darnton envisioned an electronic book in layers: "The top layer could be a concise account of the subject, available perhaps in paperback. The next layer could contain expanded versions of different aspects of the argument, not arranged sequentially as in a narrative, but as self-contained units that feed into the topmost story. The third layer could be composed of documentation. . . . A fourth layer might be historiographical. . . . A fifth layer could be pedagogic. . . . And a sixth layer could contain readers' reports, exchanges between author and editor, and letters from readers." [11] Darnton's vision, while exciting, was more archival than hypertextual. It elaborated upon the traditional book but did not change the central narrative. The book that became *In the Presence of Mine Enemies* was in fact something like what Darnton described. The book stands on its own, but a reader who goes to the Valley Project Web site will find there all the notes of the book linked directly to the primary documents to which they refer.

Will and I were thinking of something different for our article. At my urging, we tried at first to make the article as sharp a break with the past as possible. I sketched out a plan on a legal pad for a dynamic table of contents that revealed all the subunits beneath when a cursor rolled over them. Will and Kim built this interface despite some misgivings. We arrayed our writing around that elaborate mechanism and sent the Web address to Michael Grossberg to distribute to anonymous reviewers, the litmus test for scholarly publication. When the reviews came back, we could see that I had led us down a dead end. The point of the article had been to make a clear argument, but readers could not find the argument in the hypertextual jungle. We had worked to situate ourselves in the large and complex literature on slavery and sectional difference, but the fragmented exposition made that more difficult to accomplish than we had hoped. In general, the fair-minded and generous readers thought the article made demands that violated an unspoken contract. As Grossberg put it in a letter, in a traditional journal article "the author promises an argument laid out in a certain way, in a certain length, with a certain level of documentation, context, and engagement with the literature; the reader, in turn, promises to devote a certain amount of time to grappling with the article and its expected components." Our article frustrated that expectation, partly because of its length and partly because of its hypertextual form. We went back to the drawing board.

The next version of the article took a much-simplified form. Will and I returned to first principles. All professional historical writing contains three elements: argument or narrative, evidence, and the scholarly literature on the subject (also called historiography). We decided that we would build the article around those categories, linking them in what we thought would be a useful way. Kim Tryka devised tools to let the reader see where he or she was in the article and to go directly to a particular page. We kept rewriting the prose so that it would seem at ease on the computer screen. We refined the evidence and argument so that they fitted together. This time the peer reviewers thought the digital article worked about as well as such a strange form of scholarship might work. They encouraged the *American Historical Review* to publish the article, and Michael Grossberg agreed. In fact, it appeared on the cover of the print version of the journal, where a summary and introduction of the article was published. The real article of course could live only on a computer, at http://www.vcdh.virginia.edu/AHR/.

Within the article, Will and I described what we thought we had accomplished. We envisioned the article as a prism. Each module refracted evidence, argument, and historiography in a different way, shining different angles of light on the same complicated problem. We argued that slavery itself could be thought of as a prism. Slavery presented "such a difficult problem in American society because of its ability to refract nearly everything that passed through or by it. Nothing that came into either close contact or proximity to slavery was constant, nothing linear, nothing singular, nothing transparent. The form of our work and the model in which we presented it, we hoped, might most usefully approximate the historical reality we were seeking to describe." Many of the themes that appear in the other essays in this book grew out of our work in the Valley Project and out of that thesis. More important, Will won tenure in history at the University of Virginia—so far as I know, the first person ever to receive the most valuable award of academic life for work in digital history.[12]

The Valley of the Shadow Project has been an experiment to see if one of the oldest forms of learning might have a home in the electronic world growing all around us. History has traditionally been a solitary craft, the product of one person's thinking about something a long time, but the Web demands collaboration. Team-produced history makes some people nervous, as they wonder where authority and accountability lie, but the collaboration demanded by the Valley Project proved all the more satisfying for being absolutely necessary. Dozens of students and allies were pulled into the project as the archive steadily grew. We held one another accountable and found our authority in combined effort.

Many people think of history as the stories in books. This commonsensical image is misleading, however, in the same way that images of atoms as little solar systems or that pictures of evolution as profiles of ever taller and more upright apes and people are wrong. Those images all are models, radically simplified, that allow us to think about such things in the exceedingly small amounts of time that we allot to these topics in our daily lives. But to scientists, atoms appear as infinitely complex clouds of probability and evolution appears as a branching, labyrinthine bush in which some branches die out and others diversify.

Past human experience is as complex as anything in nature and likely much more so in its variability and unpredictability. Studying the past is like studying scientific processes of which we have the data but for which we cannot run the experiment again, in which there is no control, and in which we can never see the actual process we are describing and analyzing. All we have is information in various forms: words in great abundance, billions of numbers, millions of images, some sounds and buildings, artifacts.

Scientists deal with ever-increasing amounts of complex information through ever more sophisticated instruments. Historians also need to account for the complexity embedded in our information about the past. To do so, we need better instruments. Just as telescopes redefined stars and microscopes redefined cells, so might we be able to use digital tools to gain a deeper and more precise understanding of the patterns of complexity in human behavior of the past. We have only begun to try.

WHERE THE NORTH

IS THE SOUTH

IN 1995, after years of watching colleagues fly to Paris, Johannesburg, Beijing, or Bogotá for research trips and speaking engagements, I decided to apply for a posting abroad. Holding only the vaguest and most stereotyped visions, I chose the Netherlands. My application stressed, perhaps impolitely, the direct Dutch involvement in the slave trade and their connection to South African apartheid, suggesting that such commonalities with white Southerners might serve as the basis for interesting discussions of race and region.

The Fulbright Commission accepted the application and told our family we would be stationed in the city of Groningen. Though on the map it looked a bit far removed from Amsterdam and Leiden, tucked away near the North Sea, the former Fulbright chair holder in Groningen allayed our worries with his enthusiasm for the place and the people. Driving to Groningen in early March, we predictably commented on the tidiness of the small towns we passed through and admired the stone churches that dominated their centers. No tulips yet, and no one wearing wooden shoes, but it was early in the visit. Things were satisfyingly different but not alien or forbidding. We were pleased and relieved.

As we drove closer to Groningen at sundown, we studied the map: Anna Paulownastraat, our appointed address, lay near the center of town in the narrow streets of what had begun as a medieval city. We needed to gain our bearings, and to our surprise, the first convenient place to stop turned out to be a brand-new McDonald's restaurant, glowing with a familiar fluorescent sheen. Though it stood alone in an undeveloped area along the highway, the restaurant's parking lot was filled with cars and lounging teenagers. Inside, we confronted a museum of American icons: a Harley, the rear end of a pink Caddy, a life-size Marilyn, posters of Chuck, Buddy, and the King. Early rock music played on a juke-box. We had been in our adopted city for only a few minutes, and we already heard familiar accents and reassuring backbeats. Maybe this wouldn't be so hard after all, though to the astonishment of our children, the fries came covered with mayonnaise.

As we settled in, we discovered that not everything had been McDonald's-ized. Our apartment sat at the top of some satisfy-ingly European stairs, steep and narrow. Wal-Mart–like hours certainly did not rule in the Netherlands. The stores were shut-tered all Saturday afternoon, all day Sunday, and Monday morning as well, with no 7-Elevens to offer a quart of milk or loaf of bread. If you didn't have what you needed by Saturday at noon, you did without for the entire weekend. Even the Southern Baptists of our East Tennessee youth had not been so strict.

We loved the Dutchness of the things we saw but reveled in the flashes of the familiar. The television proved a big help in finding the comforts of home, since we could watch *Alf* and *The A-Team* every day, along with episodes of *The Cosby Show* and *Family Ties*. We could also see the Dukes of Hazzard careening around the California landscape that masqueraded, poorly as ever, as North Georgia. Even with Dutch subtitles across the bottom of the screen, the fake South appeared before us with a comforting regularity and with fewer commercial interruptions.

Despite such touches of home, I entered class the first day with some trepidation. What would the students know about the United States? I gained some insight when I was introduced as a visitor from the University of Virginia, and I heard a male voice in the back of the room stage-whisper that "they're in the final eight this year," referring to our men's basketball team, which had just defeated Kansas in the NCAA tournament. It turned out that a number of the students had lived in the States during high school, though none in the South, and they spoke with easy familiarity and unshakable opinions. They felt certain that the United States was 40 percent African American and that the great majority of black Americans, the Cosbys notwithstanding, lived in urban ghettos.

It soon became clear that the students felt none of the guilt I had presumed for them. They assumed no ancestral culpability for bringing the first slaves to Virginia or for supplying the Boers to South Africa. They considered racism a peculiarly American problem, one far removed from the Netherlands. The O. J. Simpson trial unfolding hourly on CNN did nothing to dislodge their certainty and their sense of their own tolerance and justice. Racism, like handguns and capital punishment, appeared to them a special American flaw, not part of a shared European ancestry.

My Dutch students and colleagues did understand regionalism, however. I came to see that they were proud and defensive about living in the north of the Netherlands. Several of them claimed ancestry from Friesland, the ancient province in the northwest of their country, and proudly demonstrated for me the unique language spoken there. They were grateful when I recognized that Holland was merely one part of their nation and that their country had a more inclusive name. They warned me when I headed to Amsterdam for meetings that people would make fun of Groningen, as indeed they did. The residents of the densely populated cities and towns of the west saw the two hours separating my university from the metropole as a distance significant in climate, culture, and sophistication. In their eyes, the north was colder and wetter, lacking in most redeeming qualities, full of empty space and cattle. It was as if the United States had been turned upside down.

I came to understand the pride behind the sign at the train station that proclaimed WELCOME TO THE NORTH. A bumper sticker on sale at the travel bureau showed a farmer wearing wooden shoes and, with a cow looking on, kicking a tourist. In case the picture wasn't clear, the slogan, in English, was: "Groningen, Love It or Leave It." Southerners who proclaim themselves "American by Birth, Southern by the Grace of God" would have recognized the spirit and admired the defiance.

Reminders of my South appeared in unexpected places in this north. I passed a tattoo parlor as I rode my bicycle to the office each day. There I could have decorated my arm with any number of Southern images, most of them involving buxom young women and a Confederate flag. One of the women was a blonde, but others bore darker skins. Two blocks away I could buy any number of Faulkner novels or books by Richard Wright. The music stores were filled with American music, the great majority of it Southern in inspiration. When the local newspapers advertised that a furniture store was presenting "The American Show," we visited it and found the same imagery we had seen in the McDonald's: lots of Elvis and Cadillacs, lots of 1950s South.

By contrast, the travel sections of the bookstores and tourism bureaus offered few Southern destinations. Pictures of New York and San Francisco dominated the covers of the U.S.A. books. Dutch visitors might want to venture to "Marlboro Country," as the dust jackets labeled the West, or Florida, which appeared as a country of its own, all beach and Disneyworld. New Orleans, quaint in its gingerbread ironworks and elderly jazzmen, constituted the only recognizably Southern place featured on the posters. While the South of the past seemed alluring, the current-day South seemed mainly a blank. The polite Dutch could find few associations to make with the South when we told them where we were from; we began to stress the proximity of Charlottesville to Washington, D.C., which brought some geographic recognition, if not admiration.

We were to find the same patterns throughout Europe. Confederate flags turned up in the piazzas of Rome; photographs of black jazz and blues greats decorated restaurants in Strasbourg; riverboat themes dominated a lounge in a hotel in France. The South was the America of the past, of the 1850s and 1860s, of the 1950s and early 1960s. The American present was California and New York.

Even race seemed disconnected from the South. To my students, African Americans appeared entirely urban, dominated by hip-hop artists and the NBA. American popular culture supplied them with no images with which to think about the South after Martin Luther King. Rather, the South appeared as shards from the past that could not be assembled into a coherent shape, alternately horrifying and romantic. John Grisham's books, it was true, were everywhere, both in English and in translation. Since corruption and a lust for money and vengeance appeared to be universal American traits, however, those books seemed set in a South little distinguished from the rest of the country. *Forrest Gump* played throughout Europe while we were there, but the homely virtues of Gump's Alabama upbringing and ultimate interracial success in the South paled in comparison with the flashy special effects that inserted him into familiar scenes of postwar American culture.

The poverty of the Southern image abroad seemed especially striking, perhaps, because I was carrying with me wherever we traveled bags of photocopies, the raw materials of what became *The Oxford Book of the American South*. The war-torn, poverty-stricken, and racially divided South testified to in those blurred and bent pages seemed far away. The testimony of Harriet Jacobs and Frederick Douglass, of Sarah Morgan and Sam Watkins, of Zora Neale Hurston and Harry Crews had no images to give them shape and place. Their lives seemed disconnected from any South that appeared on the television screens, travel posters, and album covers.

Not that the weight of the past was hard to find in the Netherlands, especially only thirty-five miles away from the German border, where Groningen lay. Eloquent monuments recalled the invasion, the Holocaust, and the sacrifice of the people of the north in World War II. Thousands of people observed ten minutes of complete silence in the city square as they recalled the liberation of the city by Canadian forces exactly fifty years before. Their quiet proved more powerful than any historical commemoration I had ever seen in the United States.

A sense of place, and the resentment, pride, and arrogance that accompany it, appeared throughout Europe just as it does in the South. If anything, that sense of place was even stronger in the Old World, more concentrated and localized, more nuanced and inflected, deeper and more bitter. Regionalism is a language that the Dutch, the Germans, the Italians, the French, and the British easily understand. They can understand the idea of the South and the war that continues to define it. But to speak across cultural boundaries in the days of mass culture is challenging. To learn from one another, we shall have to push past the billboard images of tulips and windmills, of riverboats and jazz bands, through the roar of popular culture to the real, lived history beneath.

While we lived in the Netherlands, I struggled to get a grip on the American Civil War. I had eagerly agreed to contribute to a celebratory volume for David Brion Davis, my dissertation director. But all I had was the title, "Worrying about the Civil War," because all I really knew was that I found something missing in the vast number of history books, movies, and novels on the war. As I reconstructed the evolution of American thought on the Civil War since the 1920s, I realized what it was that I missed in my own country: the sense of gravity, of terror, and of loss that I felt standing in the silent square of Groningen.

WORRYING ABOUT THE

CIVIL WAR

THE CIVIL WAR has never been more popular. Soldiers on
both sides of the war receive reverential treatment from mag-
azines that lovingly examine every facet of the war, from cavalry
to cooking, reporting on battles as if they were late-breaking
news. Reenactors gather at battlefields, getting the feel of heavy
wool clothing on a suffocating August day, of a heavy rifle, stiff
boots, and hardtack. The "Confederacy" finds no shortage of those
willing to play the role of the gallant losers. Civil War encyclopedias, atlases, biographies, sweeping surveys, and minutely detailed
volumes devoted to single days of battle fill the history sections at
bookstores in every mall in America. The business sections of those
bookstores often carry Donald T. Phillips's *Lincoln on Leadership:
Executive Strategies for Tough Times*, which proclaims that Lincoln
steered the country through the war "with a naturalness and intu-
itiveness in leading people that was [sic] at least a century ahead of
his time." Lincoln's lessons to today's executives include: "Get Out

of the Office and Circulate among the Troops" and "Keep Searching until You Find Your 'Grant.'" For the Southern point of view, the businessperson can consult *From Battlefield to Boardroom: The Leadership Lessons of Robert E. Lee*, by Bil Holton.[1]

There is no animosity in any of these historical or practical interpretations of the Civil War. It is clear that the North fought for purposes entirely good—for union and the end of slavery— but Confederate soldiers also win respect for their bravery, their devotion, and their struggle against long odds. They seem to have been playing historical roles for which they are not to blame. The reenactors, the books in the malls, and the battlefield tours generally steer clear of talking about the cause of the war, focusing instead on the common bravery and hardships of soldiers North and South. The war has become common property, with the treacherous parts helpfully roped off.

Michael Shaara's *The Killer Angels*, the most acclaimed fictional portrayal of the Civil War since *Gone with the Wind,* bears the major hallmarks of the current understanding of the war. Shaara's 1974 novel and the 1994 movie based on it, *Gettysburg,* view the conflict from the perspectives of men on both sides of the battle. We glimpse the anguish of Lee and Longstreet, the uncertainty and glory of Joshua Chamberlain, and the humanity of all involved. The moral centerpiece of both the book and the film is an Irish American Union sergeant's soliloquy on freedom and dignity. The book, like other representations of the Civil War in recent decades, combines a respect for the warriors on both sides with an idealistic vision of the war's purpose.[2]

The latest paperback edition of *The Killer Angels* carries the imprimatur of the two leading interpreters of the war. James McPherson calls Shaara's book his "favorite historical novel," and Ken Burns tells readers that the book changed his life: "I had never visited Gettysburg, knew almost nothing about that battle before I read the book, but here it all came alive." A work on the Civil War could not have more influential endorsements. McPherson's *Battle Cry of Freedom* and Burns's television series *The Civil War* have shaped the ways millions of Americans understand the central event in their nation's history. In 1988, McPherson's history of the Civil War won a Pulitzer Prize, and it remained ensconced for months at the top of the best seller list. In 1991, Burns's nine-part series attracted the largest audience ever to watch public television in the United States and became a nationwide media event. Both men have gained audiences over the years, their works becoming fixtures in the nation's libraries and classrooms. McPherson has produced a steady stream of books and essays since *Battle Cry of Freedom*, amplifying his basic tenets about the war's cause and conduct. Episodes of Burns's film are often the first sustained exposure young Americans have to the Civil War and a major influence on those who have already finished their schooling. Many people have purchased their own copies of the tapes and DVDs so they can watch them whenever they wish.[3]

Different media create different emphases, of course. Burns assembled an impressive team of academic historians to guide him, including McPherson, yet Burns is most interested in uncovering and recovering the feelings of the past. He offers an impressionistic account of the war, full of quotation, image, and sound. He focuses on the battlefields but uses private expressions of love

and grief to powerful effect. McPherson, by contrast, is a professional historian, attuned to the debates, standards, and innova-
tions of the academy. McPherson connects the military conflict to
politics and the social structures of the North and South more rig-
orously than does his counterpart.

Despite their different purposes and means, however, the
interpretations of Burns and McPherson share a perspective.
Both dramatize the ways that antislavery, progress, war, and
national identity intertwined at the time of the Civil War so that
each element became inseparable from the others. Slavery stands
as the antithesis of progress, shattering nation and creating war;
war is the means by which antislavery spreads and deepens; the
turn against slavery during the war re-creates national identity;
the new nation is freed for a more fully shared kind of progress.
This story has become common sense to Americans; emancipation, war, nation, and progress all seem part of one story, the
same story.

Both Burns and McPherson make sophisticated use of their
preferred medium. Burns explains the coming of the war in just a
few minutes of his long film, introducing the cotton gin and portraying the resulting conflicts as the inevitable result of the
growth of slavery. Familiar faces and events flash past, from
William Lloyd Garrison to Frederick Douglass to Harriet
Beecher Stowe to Abraham Lincoln, from Bleeding Kansas to
Harpers Ferry to Fort Sumter. McPherson, by contrast, spends
hundreds of pages explaining the origins of the war. Like Burns,
McPherson uses quotation extensively and effectively; he lets the
words of his protagonists carry his story. Persuasive Northern

speakers come in at key points to make the liberal and nationalist statements attractive to McPherson.

White Northerners, white Southerners, and black Americans all grow morally during the war that Burns and McPherson portray. The white North comes truly to abhor slavery; white Southerners recognize the limits of their power and the meaning of full nationhood; black Americans gain not only freedom but also heightened dignity when they take up arms for their freedom. Abraham Lincoln embodies this moral growth of his nation, as the slaughter on the battlefield gradually persuades the cautious president that the war must become a war against slavery. Lincoln's transformation represents that of the North as a whole, and his assassination brings the story to its end.[4]

Burns and McPherson hold up the story of the Civil War as an inspiration to Americans of today. As Burns puts it, "If there's one political theme in this film, it's this: The Civil War is a chronicle of making permanent that which was promised, but not delivered, in the Declaration of Independence and the Constitution." McPherson, long known as a historian of abolitionism, stresses that the war was about freedom in its many manifestations. "Lincoln led the country through the worst of times to a triumph that left America stronger, more free, and more democratic," he has written recently. "And that offers a lesson not only for Americans but also for 'the whole family of man.'" These historians celebrate the outcome of a war that put the country on the long path to the civil rights movement and greater equality. Their powerful histories tell a story of freedom emerging through the trial of war, of a great nation becoming greater through suffering.[5]

Despite the harrowing picture of war in Burns's film, where severed limbs and bleaching bones appear frequently and memorably, his North and South are engaged in a collaborative effort. "Between 1861 and 1865, Americans made war on each other and killed each other in great numbers—" Burns's narrator, David McCullough, tells viewers early in the film, "if only to become the kind of country that could no longer conceive of how that was possible." The beginning and the end of the war fuse into one; the soldiers kill one another for the common purpose of discovering the depth and the nature of their nationalism. The final scene in Burns's epic shows footage from 1913, when aging veterans of Gettysburg return to the scenes of carnage to stroll peacefully together through fields now regrown green and alive. McPherson has less of a reconciliationist bent than Burns, but he uses the first page of his book to emphasize that versions of the song "The Battle Cry of Freedom" were popular in both the North and the South. His title is nonpartisan.[6]

Burns and McPherson work hard to protect the memory of the war. They defend its integrity from the evasions of those who insist that the South fought for something other than slavery; they protect it from those who emphasize the North's narrow self-interest; they protect it from the many historians who hold military history in disdain; they protect it from cynics on both the right and the left. For Burns and McPherson, the war's sacrifices must not be wasted; the people of the United States must not become unaware and unappreciative of what was at stake and what was won. McPherson continually reminds Americans, as his recent book titles put it, "what they fought for," that "we cannot escape history," that Lincoln led "the second American Revolution," and that soldiers fought "for cause and comrades." He has spearheaded efforts to protect battlefields, "sacred soil," from development.

McPherson is so vigilant because he recognizes that this interpretation has become established only after long struggle. The elegance and directness with which he and Burns tell their stories can lead us to forget what a complicated event the Civil War was. It was, after all, simultaneously a war among citizens and among states, a war fought by disciplined soldier-citizens and a war that continually threatened to spin out of anyone's control, a war whose opponents were driven by hatred yet quickly reconciled when it became convenient, a war in which slavery died at the hands of soldiers who often fought against slavery reluctantly and even then because slavery's destruction seemed the only practical way to win. The current interpretations contain these tensions in an overarching story of emergent freedom and reconciliation. While acknowledging the complicated decisions people faced, Burns and McPherson resolve them through narrative. White Northerners, including Lincoln, announce early on that the war is not about slavery, but the words do not disturb us because we know these people change their minds later on. White Southerners claim plausible support from the Constitution, but their arguments have little weight because they lose the war and thus their arguments. Black Americans denounce the war at first as irrelevant or worse, but we know they are fortunately mistaken.

So self-evident does the dominant interpretation seem that many Americans of today never suspect how hotly historians have contested these issues throughout much of the twentieth century. While vestiges of older interpretations still crop up in people's vague recollections, no one has stepped forward in a very long time to offer a popularly accepted counterargument to the explanation codified in Burns and McPherson. Major American thinkers last offered strong dissent three decades ago, when Robert Penn Warren and Edmund Wilson expressed visions of the Civil War that now seem startling in their vehemence and skepticism. Wilson made audacious comparisons in his influential book *Patriotic Gore*, a survey of wartime writing. "All animals must prey on some form of life that they can capture, and all will eat as much as they can," Wilson dryly observed as he compared the North and the South to sea slugs he had seen in a Walt Disney documentary. Man is different only because he "has succeeded in cultivating enough of what he calls 'morality' and 'reason' to justify what he is doing in terms of what he calls 'virtue' and 'civilization.'" Abraham Lincoln, Wilson thought, should be grouped with other leaders who sought to build nations through force and appeal to transcendent meaning, Bismarck and Lenin.[7]

Robert Penn Warren offered a more generous yet still critical meditation in his book *The Legacy of the Civil War*. The war, Warren cautioned, produced two dangerous habits of mind in Americans. For the South, it offered "The Great Alibi," the great excuse for everything that was wrong or lacking in the region. For the North, it offered "The Treasury of Virtue," in which the war appeared as "a consciously undertaken crusade so full of righteousness that there is enough overplus stored in Heaven, like the deeds of the saints, to take care of all the small failings and oversights of the descendants of the crusaders, certainly unto the present generation." Warren, like Wilson, did not shun dramatic effect. It was tempting, he argued, for Americans to regard the war as "part of our divinely instituted success story, and to think, in some shadowy corner of the mind, of the dead at Gettysburg as a small price to pay for the development of a really satisfactory and cheap compact car with decent pick-up and road-holding capability."[8]

Wilson and Warren wrote during the one hundredth anniversary of the war—"this absurd centennial," Wilson called it—when histories, plays, reenactments, products, and commemorations of all sorts proliferated. Wilson and Warren wrote to dampen the self-righteousness and materialism to which Americans inclined in those stressful years of the cold war. The two authors considered themselves voices in the wilderness, delivering jeremiads, for a once-powerful tradition of skepticism about the Civil War had crumbled and a new tradition of acceptance and celebration was rising in its place.[9]

The skeptical viewpoint had peaked decades earlier, in the 1920s and 1930s, when revisionism flourished. The revisionists challenged the comforting bargain put forward in the years before World War I by Southern journalists such as Henry Grady and scholars such as Woodrow Wilson. Without sacrificing any respect for the Lost Cause, the reconciliationist bargain admitted that secession had been a mistake and that the nation should never have been divided. It argued that emancipation had been a fortunate occurrence for the white South, to which slavery had been a burden. Southerners who made such concessions won in return the

admission by white Northerners that Reconstruction and its elevation of black Southerners had been a mistake. This understanding
of the Civil War, in other words, was simultaneously antislavery
and racist, emphasizing the triumph of white reconciliation and
progress at the expense of black rights. All white people emerged
from the conflict looking high-minded and principled.[10]

Charles and Mary Beard's immensely popular *The Rise of
American Civilization*, first published in 1927 and reflecting the disillusionment that followed World War I, scoffed at this interpretation. They argued that neither side had been high-minded, that the
Civil War had been fought over neither slavery nor states' rights.
Rather, economic issues had stood paramount. "If the southern
planters had been content to grant tariffs, bounties, subsidies, and
preferences to northern commerce and industry," the Beards
declared, "it is not probable that they would have been molested
in their most imperious proclamations of sovereignty." The skeptical view broadened and deepened throughout the 1930s. In
1939, Avery Craven's *The Repressible Conflict* argued that the Civil
War should be judged by its consequences and that those consequences looked bleak indeed at the end of the 1930s. The black
American had escaped "little of the hard fate destined for his race
in 1850. Industrial capitalism, with the banners of righteousness,
patriotism, and progress over its head and with all critics hushed in
disgrace and defeat, went on to its fullness and perhaps its ruin."
Something precious had been lost in the Civil War, Craven
lamented: "a Constitution which might have protected rights, an
agrarian way of life which might have fostered a rich American
culture and a sane economic order, a decentralized government

wherein individuals and localities might have realized a more satisfactory democracy." Craven believed, along with many Americans,
that those dreams had died with the Civil War.[11]

In 1940, James G. Randall delivered his presidential address to
the leading organization of historians of the United States. The
address, entitled "The Blundering Generation," concluded that "the
Civil War mind seems a sorry *mélange* of party bile, crisis melo-
drama, inflated eloquence, unreason, religious fury, self-righteousness, unctuous self-deception, and hate."The war could, and should,
have been avoided, Randall argued, for it was not fought over irreconcilable differences between the North and South. Randall, like
his fellow revisionists, thought he was moving discussion of the war
to more realistic grounds, puncturing Northern arrogance and
Southern apology.The Civil War was not to be glorified. It stood as
an example of how democratic politics could run out of control, of
the way moral absolutism could blind people to their own faults and
to the consequences of their actions.[12]

Such claims did not go completely uncontested, for black historians warned that such views distorted all American history.
Throughout the Gilded Age, abolitionists such as Frederick
Douglass, trying to create a usable past, argued in vain that the
war had been fought over slavery. In 1935, during the peak of
revisionism, W. E. B. DuBois argued that the Beards' work created
the "comfortable feeling that nothing right or wrong is involved.
Manufacturing and industry develop in the North; agrarian feu-
dalism develops in the South. They clash, as winds and waters
strive, and the stronger forces develop the tremendous industrial
machine that governs us so magnificently and selfishly today."

DuBois wondered how "anyone who reads the *Congressional Globe* from 1850 to 1860, the lives of contemporary statesmen and public characters, North and South, the discourses in the newspapers and accounts of meetings and speeches, [could] doubt that Negro slavery was the cause of the Civil War." DuBois granted that the "North went to war without the slightest idea of freeing the slave" but showed how the abolitionists and the slaves themselves forced Lincoln into making the war one against slavery. These arguments won little attention or respect from white historians. This was the heyday of revisionism; "everyone" knew the war had been a mistake.[13]

Yet revisionism, so powerful in the first half of the twentieth century, faded away with remarkable speed in the second half. No sooner had World War II ended than commentators called for a rethinking of the dominant skeptical interpretation of the Civil War. Arthur Schlesinger, Jr., argued in 1949 that the revisionists, despite their claims to the contrary, had been "sentimentalists," insensitive to the evil of slavery and excessively squeamish about using violence to end it. "The unhappy fact is that man occasionally works himself into a log-jam; and that log-jam must be burst by violence," Schlesinger lectured. "We know that well enough from the experience of the last decade." In 1953, the year that James Randall died, the black historian Benjamin Quarles published *The Negro in the Civil War*, arguing that black people had played central roles in transforming the Civil War into a war to end slavery. Avery Craven began toning down his earlier views, and no one picked up the revisionist banner. David Donald, a student of Randall's who, more than any other leading scholar, seemed sympathetic to the revisionists, explained in 1960 why the perspective no longer won converts: "To those who reached maturity during the years when irresistible and complex forces brought the United States, and the whole civilized world, into a disastrous world war, it no longer seems so simple to unravel the causes of the conflict and to pass out praise and blame like honors at a college commencement exercise."[14]

The decline of revisionism was part of a larger rethinking of the American past. Historians in the 1960s, 1970s, and 1980s changed the way Americans understood nineteenth-century America, reflecting the influence of the civil rights movement, the war on poverty, and the counterculture. Many of the country's most visible historians valued rapid reform, through non-electoral means if necessary, far more than they did the political stability, gradual change, and regional compromise championed by the revisionists. A self-consciously reformist, often radical social history swept the profession, displaying and analyzing evidence of injustice and dominion. Southern slaves emerged as fully human, anguished by their bondage and determined to be free in whatever ways they could. Abolitionists no longer appeared to be deluded zealots but rather men and women willing to risk their lives for the highest religious and political ideals. The Republicans came to be seen primarily as advocates of free labor and economic progress, hating the South for its political arrogance and its violation of American virtues. Politicians in general no longer appeared to be blundering but responding, and rather timorously at that, to the very real dilemmas of their society.[15]

Despite penetrating essays and books by historians attentive to the complexities of the party system, no aggressive Civil War revisionism swept over America in the 1960s. This absence of anti-war thinking is surprising. After all, if the disappointments following World War I helped create the first revisionism, why did the far greater disillusionment with the war in Vietnam not create another surge of revisionism? Although disgust with the military and with warfare, with claims of national virtue and innocence, permeated the academy in the late 1960s and early 1970s, only one young scholar, a graduate student, issued a call for "a new revisionism." In 1969 he argued that "the limited improvement in the status of the Negro in this country was not worth the expenditure in lives required to make that improvement possible."[16]

Merely to quote the argument today is to show why it did not succeed: The antiwar spirit directly conflicted with the other great ideal of the sixties, black freedom. Revisionists in the 1920s and 1930s had argued that the end of slavery was not worth six hundred thousand lives because those historians did not consider slavery much worse than what followed. By the late 1960s, however, slavery seemed so uniquely and undeniably wrong that the calculus of sacrifice had changed. The moral passion that earlier generations had invested in explaining why there should have been no Civil War now focused on explaining why the war and Reconstruction had not been more thorough, why Reconstruction had not been more aggressively supported by confiscation and military power. Scholars' compassion now focused more on the former slaves than on the soldiers in the war. The war itself became something of a scholarly backwater, neglected by the leading historians of nineteenth-century America. The distaste for the war in

Vietnam manifested itself in an aversion to any kind of military history, while the fascination with social history made generals and their maneuvers seem irrelevant and boring at best.

Scholars, if not interested in the events on the battlefields, did remain intrigued by the causes of the Civil War. To scholars mindful of either mainstream social science or Marxist thought, the North increasingly appeared as a modern and modernizing society locked in an unavoidable struggle with an antimodern, archaic, and stagnant slave South. The economic conflict between the two societies no longer seemed one merely of tariffs and taxes, issues that could have been worked out, but rather a fundamental clash of free labor and slavery, of the future and the past. The two societies, historians of widely differing perspectives came to agree, could not, should not have coexisted within the same nation-state. Slavery had to be destroyed as soon as possible, and given the white South's intransigence, only violence was likely to accomplish that purpose.[17]

By the 1970s and 1980s, in sum, the Civil War no longer manifested itself as a moral problem to the people who wrote the major books about the struggle. Such authors wasted little ink on what had been lost in the war other than precious lives; they worried little about how the war might have been avoided. Slavery displaced other questions that had long agitated Americans, questions about state power, about centralization, about democracy, about war itself. The Civil War came to seem like bitter medicine the country had to swallow for its own good.

Today's stories pivot around moments of wartime cohesion, purposefulness, and decision, especially the growing recognition among white Northerners that the war had to be a war to end slavery, not merely one to save the Union. The war stands as a crucible that burned away the impurities in the Union purpose; this is what Americans were willing to die for, the story says, this is how America atoned for the sin of slavery. The Civil War appears as the origins of our better selves, of the time when we threw off the slavery of our inheritance and became truly American. To Ken Burns, the war marked the equivalent of a "traumatic event in our childhood." To James McPherson, a generous reckoning of the war's purposes and consequences can help Americans overcome "the climate of disillusionment produced by the Vietnam War and the aftermath of the civil rights movement."[18]

So what is wrong with a generous interpretation? After all, it puts the ideals of democracy and nationhood at the center of the story, offering a counterweight to those who have appealed to less expansive interpretations of the nation's ideals. It holds up heroes worth emulating. It reconciles the North and South to each other, giving respect where it has not always been found. It places the struggle for black freedom and equality at the heart of American history. It connects Americans with their past. All these worthy purposes have been won only after great effort, and a person of goodwill might think twice before questioning them. Yet if we do not question them, we close ourselves off from other kinds of understanding, other perspectives on the American nation.

The current interpretation reassures Americans by reconciling the great anomaly of slavery with an overarching story of a people devoted to liberty. These stories reassure Americans by reconciling the horrors of fratricidal war with a vision of a peace-loving republic devoted to democracy and prosperity. They tell the story of a devastating war so that it seems not merely unavoidable but transformative and ultimately healing. The stories help restock Robert Penn Warren's "Treasury of Virtue" in the wake of the war in Vietnam. White Southerners have been permitted limited access to parts of the treasury, handed the keys to the rooms that contain honor, bravery, and even idealism—though not justice. Black Americans have finally been acknowledged as agents in their own freedom. But it is white Northern men who come off best in these stories, martyrs for union and the liberty of others.[19]

The new interpretation contains little of the cynicism and irony of the revisionists of the 1920s and 1930s. Today's stories tend to be earnest accounts, clear and linear, with motives and emotions close to the surface. Indeed, it is in part the very appeal of their stories as stories that makes them so resistant to revision, that makes them seem so self-evident. The accounts of the war have a familiar narrative shape; they present an apparently unre-solvable problem and then, after great trials, show its resolution, echoing other basic stories of Western and American culture.

We understand the plot lines of war, dramatized every day on sports fields and in action films: good causes and bad ones, cowardice and bravery, sacrifice and glory, winners and losers, sudden victories and unexpected reverses. Fundamental ideas of history, religion, and science, as Hannah Arendt has argued, incline twentieth-century people to see wars as major engines of beneficial social change even as we loathe and fear the conflict itself. Not only does the Judeo-Christian religious tradition accustom us to think of violence and blood as necessary accompaniments of progress, but evolutionism leads us to conceive of violence as a part of nature, a way for bad ideas and institutions to be culled. These assumptions, combined with a widespread belief in the divine favor enjoyed by the United States, have made it easy for Americans to believe that the Civil War was not merely necessary but actually good for the country in the long run.[20]

Our current understanding of the war makes us impatient with those in the North—the great majority, at the beginning—who argued that they were fighting only for union, not for the end of bondage. We are befuddled by black Northerners who argued that a war fought to protect the Union—"this unholy, ill-begotten, would-be Republican government, that summons all its skill, energy, and might, of money, men, and false philosophy that a corrupt nation can bring to bear, to support, extend, and perpetuate that vilest of all vile systems, American slavery"—was not a war worth fighting. We are disappointed with those many white men who died for the Union who would not willingly have risked their lives for the end of slavery. As the *Chicago Times,* commenting on Lincoln's Gettysburg Address, put it, "They were men possessing too much self-respect to declare that negroes were their equals, or were entitled to equal privileges."[21]

Garry Wills's *Lincoln at Gettysburg* (1992) used such quotations to explain the great transformation of the North. Wills, in his best-selling and prizewinning interpretation of the war, argued that Lincoln, in the mere 272 words of the address, cleared "the infected atmosphere of American history itself, tainted with official sins and inherited guilt." Rather than burn the Constitution because it countenanced slavery, as William Lloyd Garrison had proposed, Lincoln instead "altered the document from within, by appeal from its letter to the spirit, subtly changing the recalcitrant stuff of that legal compromise, bringing it to its own indictment." Lincoln's redefinition of the Constitution to embrace black equality, Wills admiringly noted, was "one of the most daring acts of open-air sleight of hand ever witnessed by the unsuspecting. Everyone in that vast throng of thousands was having his or her intellectual pocket picked. The crowd departed with a new thing in its ideological luggage, that new constitution Lincoln had substituted for the one they brought with them."[22] Lincoln tricked Americans into being better than they really were, into fighting for a higher cause. Wills's Lincoln transmogrified a war for union into a war for freedom.

There are of course scholarly dissenters from this standard interpretation. Historians such as David Potter, J. Mills Thornton, Michael Holt, William Gienapp, and William Freehling have questioned the political narrative that makes the conflict over slavery seem relatively straightforward, in either the North or the South. Their regions are marked by strong countercurrents, compromises, and possibilities for alignments other than those that brought on the war.[23] Other historians have argued that African Americans did more to free themselves than Abraham Lincoln ever did. In the eyes of Leon Litwack, Ira Berlin, Barbara Fields, and others, the focus on white Northern soldiers and civilians gives undue credit to reluctant friends of freedom. Without the desperate efforts by slaves to free themselves, they argue, the Union cause would have remained a cause for union alone. It was anonymous African Americans who forced the hands of Union generals, who forced them to take a stand on slavery, who forced them to recognize that only by ending slavery could the North win the war. Assuming an implicit and intrinsic push toward freedom on the part of the North, these historians warn, gives that society far too much moral credit. [24]

Other historians have recently argued that the conflict was considerably more vindictive, hateful, and destructive than the new orthodoxy emphasizes. Michael Perman, Charles Royster, Michael Fellman, and Steven Ash stress the chaotic violence that swirled around the regimented violence of the war, that tormented the border regions from Missouri to occupied South Carolina, that ravaged the postwar period throughout the South and nullified much that the war claimed to have won. Noncombatants as well as leading generals, these historians show, were often less eager to rejoin the foe in union than to see them dead. As Royster puts it, Northerners and Southerners fell into "visions of purgation and redemption, into anticipation and intuition and spiritual apotheosis, into bloodshed that was not only intentional pursuit of interests of state but was also sacramental, erotic, mystical, and strangely gratifying." Such imagery has little place in the way most Americans today prefer to remember the war, where violence was inflicted almost reluctantly, brother against brother. [25]

The dominant story of the war can absorb a great deal of such amendment, however, without changing its fundamental outlines. The standard interpretation, after all, never makes the war seem painless; in fact, the suffering, struggle, conflict, and uncertainty constitute crucial parts of the "ordeal by fire" that tried the nation and its ideals. Arguments about the complexities of the antebellum period can complicate without undermining a belief that the war, as Lincoln put it, was "somehow" about slavery. Arguments that Southern slaves helped free themselves can fit into, even enrich a story of the war that emphasizes the growth of liberty. Though arguments about the irrationality, brutality, and bloodthirstiness of the war may signal a new, darker school of interpretation, defenders of the standard interpretation have argued that the American Civil War actually saw less inhumanity than most other wars, that the American war was distinguished by the rigor with which soldiers and leaders played by agreed-upon rules. Even historians find it hard, in other words, to convey an overall interpretation of the war that fundamentally challenges the one that has become so deeply entrenched in American culture.[26]

This lack of far-reaching debate over the Civil War—so unlike that which has surrounded other major historical events, such as the French Revolution, the Holocaust, and the Cold War—may not be a cause for self-congratulation. It is not merely that all the evidence is in and accounted for, that historians have finally found the one true interpretation. It may be, rather, that we like the current story too much to challenge it very deeply and that we foreclose questions by repeating familiar formulas. The risk of our apparent consensus is that we paper over the complicated moral issues raised by a war that left hundreds of thousands of people dead. The risk is that we no longer worry about the Civil War.

The American Civil War presents great narrative opportunities. No one could ask for a richer subject, a better plot line of conflict and resolution, struggle and triumph, good and evil. But with those opportunities also come temptations. All the struggle, conflict, and uncertainty can appear as so many plot complications in a story that drives to its natural conclusion. Because the secession conflict led to the Civil War, war now seems to be the intention of those who sought to leave the Union. Because the war became a bloodbath of incalculable scale, that scale now seems inevitable. Because the war ended with the survival of the Union, that survival now seems the natural outcome of the war. Because slavery came to an end in 1865, that victory has suffused the purposes of the North throughout the war and before. The story has been settled upon, assuming the shape of an elaborate play. Every American schoolchild learns the set pieces, the way that generals and presidents personified various traits: Grant's cool purposefulness, Lee's selfless dedication to homeland, Sherman's prescient destructiveness, Lincoln's forgiveness and suffering.

Yet things may not have been so settled. The contingencies of the war, we might recognize, could easily have changed not only the outcome of the conflict but its apparent moral meaning as well. If the North had overwhelmed the South in 1862, the victory would have brought the restoration of the Union without the immediate end of slavery. If that had happened, the war's causes as well as its outcome would be understood differently today. Similarly, if Lincoln had escaped assassination and overseen the conciliatory form of reconstruction he apparently had in mind, he would not seem the transcendental visionary he seems now. Not only events were contingent, in other words, but so were apparently fixed ideologies, values, personalities, and memories. With one key victory, after all, George McClellan might well be pictured on classroom walls throughout a very different kind of United States.[27]

We might rethink too the role of modernity in causing and deciding the war. Modernity is perhaps the single most deeply embedded part of the standard story; Americans of all regions and generations, for different reasons, accept the idea that the North was a modern society that could not long coexist with a South that had rejected modernity. James McPherson, for example, divides the country into two halves with different orientations toward "modernization." He characterizes that process as one marked by "an evolution from the traditional, rural, village-oriented system of personal and kinship ties, in which status is 'ascriptive' (inherited), toward a fluid, cosmopolitan, impersonal, and pluralistic society, in which status is achieved by merit." A recent book that offers "everything you need to know about America's greatest conflict but never learned" boils things down this way: "The America of the Union states was racing toward the twentieth century, with banks, booming factories, railroads, canals, and steamship lines. . . . The southern states of the Confederacy were, in many respects, standing still in time." A prominent historian has argued that a modern society such as the North, in conflict with a nonmodern or less modern society such as the South, will benefit from modernity in wartime because "its greater social mobility and emphasis on achievement will bring to the fore more effective leaders, and its more highly differentiated structure of social and occupational roles will make possible a more efficient allocation of tasks."[28]

Such views may give modernity more credit than it deserves as the driving force behind freedom and military victory. Modern economies, after all, have often found ways to make their peace with nondemocratic government, coercive labor, and constrained liberties. Moreover, while the events of the twentieth century show that a technologically sophisticated, "highly differentiated" society can become a terrifyingly effective war machine, Americans have learned that more advanced societies do not always triumph over less developed enemies. If the South had in fact won the Civil War historians could plausibly argue that a defensive, highly mobilized, self-sacrificing, organic South would naturally defeat the commercial, aggressive, polyglot, individualistic North, with its draft riots, paid substitutes, and indecisive president. They would look to the American Revolution as foreshadowing the inevitable success of the Confederacy, just as the Confederates themselves did.

Even this counterfactual perspective does not go far enough, for it neglects how "modern" the slave South itself had become by the late antebellum period. This topic has been hotly debated by historians for decades, revealing that modernity is among the most slippery of concepts, especially as it related to slavery. It seems fair to say that from the perspective of most other societies in the world in 1860 the slave South was an advanced society, rich in the machinery and trappings of modernity. Railroads, telegraphs, cities, newspapers, active political parties, factories, and reform societies had emerged in the 1840s and 1850s. Slavery grew no weaker as a result, however, showing itself dismayingly adaptable. Where the incentives existed, as in Virginia, slaves were put to work in the machinery of the new age, laboring in such industries as iron foundries. White Southerners considered themselves a progressive people, taking the best of the new while maintaining social stability and responsibility for their workers. They prided themselves on their white democracy, their widespread church membership, and their strict adherence to the Constitution. They saw themselves on a different, smoother, more humane path to progress, the obvious brutality and inhumanity of slavery notwithstanding.[29]

Modernity, slavery, and nation appeared in strange combinations in the secession crisis and war. Some of the largest planters and richest slave areas in the deep South tended to be Unionist, while cities, where modern ways had made the greatest inroads in the slave South, often voted for secession. The machinery of print and telegraph, rather than moderate city dwellers' opinions and incline them toward freedom, could inflame them against the North. The most heavily Unionist districts, for their part, were those least connected to the South and the rest of the nation; upcountry people seemed bound to older ideas of nation, not newer ones. Once the war began, the Confederacy innovated quickly on the battlefield, on the oceans, and behind the lines, even as it held stubbornly to slavery.

There is no doubt that the North was more economically developed than the South and that slavery rendered the South economically backward by comparison. But seeing the war as a conflict between the future and the past tempts us to think that modernity naturally, if often violently, creates freedom. It tempts us to bifurcate and simplify the causes of the war into easy-to-understand formulas that flatter Americans, including white

Southerners, into thinking that things unfolded pretty much as they were destined to unfold. It conflates slavery with the agrarian past and ignores the viruslike ability of slavery to insinuate itself into diverse kinds of societies. An interpretation based on modernization ignores how intertwined North and South, black and white, slavery and freedom were in antebellum America.

Slavery and freedom remain the keys to understanding the war, but they are the place to begin our questions, not to end them. The interpretation of the Civil War that appeals to so many Americans today weaves antislavery, war, economic progress, and nationalism into an inseparable whole. Freedom, it seems, was driven by the machinery of modern life, achieved through cathartic violence, and embodied in a government that valued freedom above all else. The triumph, moreover, seems to have operated retroactively. A nation that tolerated slavery at its founding can seem, in retrospect, fundamentally opposed to slavery. A national economy that for generations depended on slavery as its mainspring can seem intrinsically antagonistic to slavery. A war that began as a fight to maintain the Union with strong protections for slavery can be seen as inherently antislavery from the beginning. Given these assumptions, a conflagration on the scale of the Civil War appears inevitable.

Those who resist this argument, its assumptions, and its implications are often conservatives of various kinds. Some are white Southerners unwilling, as they see it, to abandon their ancestors and their heritage. Other critics resent the power of the national government and are jealous for the power of states and localities.[30] Others are racists, denying to black Americans the freedoms and aspirations available to other Americans. As a result, liberals have stood staunchly behind the standard interpretation, hoping it can help strengthen the activism and authority of the national government, the claims of African Americans for full citizenship, and the tradition of white reform.

Perhaps, however, the standard interpretation is no longer serving liberal ends as it once did. The story of the Civil War has become a story of things being settled, of scores being righted. Movies and books that tell of Americans killing more than six hundred thousand other Americans somehow convey a sense of the greatness of everyone concerned and of the nation for which they died. Such faith in the transformative effects of warfare can make it easier for Americans to find other wars natural and inevitable. Celebrating the martyrdom of whites for black freedom can reduce white guilt. Celebrating the bravery of Confederate soldiers and the brilliance of Confederate generals can trivialize the stakes of the war. Celebrating sectional reconciliation can mask the struggles over justice, power, and arrogance that have marked relations between the North and South for generations.

A new Civil War revisionism may help us avoid some of these temptations. That revisionism, unlike its predecessors, might focus on the way we relate the Civil War rather than on matters of interpretation alone. It might resist the very notion of the war as a single story, with a beginning, middle, and end, with turning points and near misses. The war did not have a single chronology, a rising and falling, an obvious pivot, but rather competing and intertwining chronologies in different theaters, on different home fronts, in politics and in economies. The sequence of sectional crisis, war, and aftermath did not follow a cumulative and linear development. To some, war seemed less impending in 1859 than in 1854, less threatening in February 1861 than in November 1860. The war seemed more pointedly about slavery in late 1863 than it did six months later, when the presidential election in the North threatened to capsize the Lincoln administration. Black freedom promised more liberation in 1865 than it had delivered by 1876.

A new revisionism might also set aside the Olympian perspective and voice of our dominant books and films to provide a different sense of the war's depth and scale. It might give up older reassurances to provide new kinds of clarity. It might convey what Stephen Crane's *The Red Badge of Courage* conveyed: the swirl of action and reflection, the partial knowledge of those swept up in war. A new revisionism might inspire battle histories that leave some of the fog of battle on the page.

A new revisionism would place more distance between nineteenth-century Americans and us, the very distance that lets us see ourselves more clearly. If Americans resist the temptation to count every cost of the Civil War as a "sacrifice," we might be more grateful for our simple good fortune and perhaps less self-satisfied with the people we have become. If we acknowledge that we inherit all of the past and not merely those parts we like to call our "heritage," we would better respect the past's complexity, weight, and importance. If we recognize that the Civil War did not represent the apotheosis of American ideals, we might look for that culmination in the future rather than in the past. All we need is the faith to approach these threatening years without a comforting story already in hand.

WHAT CAUSED THE

CIVIL WAR?

On *The Simpsons*, a popular animated satire of American life, Apu Nahasapeemapetilan, an industrious South Asian immigrant in Springfield, U.S.A., has studied hard for his citizenship test. "What was the cause of the Civil War?" is the final question on the oral quiz. "Actually, there were numerous causes," says Apu. "Aside from the obvious schism between the abolitionists and the anti-abolitionists, there were economic factors, both domestic and inter—" The official, clearly bored with such superfluous erudition, intones flatly: "Just say slavery." Apu eagerly concedes the point: "Slavery it is, sir." With this declaration Apu wins his American citizenship.[1]

Why is this funny? It's not because slavery was *not* the cause of the Civil War, but because the bureaucrat demands a rote answer to explain a profoundly complex problem at the center of the nation's experience. Some Americans of course have other short explanations for the Civil War. "It was really just economics," one often hears, or "it was really about states' rights" or "Southerners just wanted to be left alone with their way of life." People deliver these explanations with an air of savvy common sense, of putting the matter to rest.

Historians are exasperated by such assertions. No respected historian has argued for decades that the Civil War was fought over tariffs, that abolitionists were mere hypocrites, or that only constitutional concerns drove secession. Nor does any historian argue that white Northerners, suddenly discovering that slavery was a gross injustice to African Americans, rose up in 1861 to sacrifice 350,000 of their sons, brothers, and fathers to emancipate the slaves. Yet one still hears the old explanations in virtually any discussion of the Civil War.

The challenge of explaining the Civil War has led historians to seek clarity in two ways of thought. One school, the fundamentalists, emphasizes the intrinsic, inevitable conflict between slavery and free labor. The other, the revisionists, emphasizes discrete events and political structures rather than slavery itself. Both sides see crucial parts of the problem, but it has proved difficult to reconcile the perspectives because they approach the Civil War with different assumptions about what drives history.[2] One focuses on deep social and cultural structures, the other on public events close in time and consequence to the war's beginning. Both perspectives see essential aspects of the problem, but neither sees it whole.

Fundamentalists claim with confidence that the Civil War was a struggle over the future of the United States and can say with justice that the war pitted slavery against freedom. Revisionists can truthfully say that the Civil War was caused by the disintegration of the Democrats, the failure of compromise, and the election of Abraham Lincoln. For the fundamentalists, slavery is front and center; for the revisionists, slavery is buried beneath layers of white ideology and politics. As thousands of books and articles show, both schools have a point.

"What caused the Civil War?" misleads us because it seems such a straightforward question. The implication of "what" is that some factor can be isolated, held apart from everything else. "Cause" evokes a mechanical model of action and reaction. "The" implies that the Civil War was the four-year set of battles and outcomes that eventually unfolded, including Union victory and emancipation. Such a simple question virtually demands a simple answer.

We really need a series of questions that combine the structural explanation of the fundamentalists with the dynamic explanation of the revisionists. The questions should acknowledge that what became the Civil War was caused over and over again as it changed from a political conflict to a military conflict to a struggle over emancipation. We need to set aside our knowledge of later events and their outcome to ask the first key question: "What motivated millions of Americans to declare themselves as enemies of one another in 1859, in 1860, and in 1861?" We must push below the surface of familiar events to see how people throughout the social order thought of themselves and their responsibilities.

The Civil War came by a number of small steps, each with an explicit logic all its own. Combined, these small steps led to large unanticipated consequences. Each period in the struggle between 1859 and 1861, despite recurring language and personalities, was framed differently, presented different challenges, permitted different solutions, and pushed toward different outcomes. The frame of perception and decision making before John Brown differed from that which followed; that frame changed again when the parties put four candidates in the field, again when Lincoln won the Republican nomination, again when Lincoln won the election, again when the Gulf South states seceded, again when Fort Sumter was fired upon and the troops were called out. Each frame dictated the range of actions, and those ranges grew ever more restricted with each stage.

Slavery was a profound economic, political, religious, and moral problem, the most profound the nation has ever faced. But that problem did not lead to war in a rational, predictable way. The war came through misunderstanding, confusion, miscalculation. Both sides underestimated the location of fundamental loyalty in the other. Both received incorrect images of the other in the partisan press. Political belief distorted each side's view of the other's economy and class relations. Both sides believed the other was bluffing, both believed that the other's internal differences and conflicts would lead it to buckle, and both believed they had latent but powerful allies in the other region that would prevent war. By the time people made up their minds to fight, slavery itself had become obscured. Southern white men did not fight for slavery; they fought for a new nation built on slavery. White Northerners did not fight to end slavery; they fought to defend the integrity of their nation. Yet slavery, as Abraham Lincoln later put it, "somehow" drove everything.

What we might call "deep contingency" can help explain this

puzzle. All social life is "contingent," implicated and unpredictable, because all parts of life depend on one another. What we think of as public and private, economic and political, religious and secular, and military and civilian are deeply connected. Social change can start anywhere and lead anywhere. As a result, the most profound kinds of self-understanding can change radically and abruptly. The American Civil War stands as an example of how history can suddenly pivot and take a new direction. Histories of other nations in other times record similar seismic changes, changes explainable only through deep contingency.

An argument for deep contingency is based on the simple principle that the best explanation reckons with the most information. Simple explanations that ignore complication in an impatient determination to get to a bottom line or root cause are worse than useless. They give the false impression that we have explained something when we have not.

Those who want a demographic explanation for the Civil War, for example, make the point that the higher the percentage of slaves in Southern states, the greater the eagerness with which those states seceded. The deep South had a higher percentage of slaves, and the deep South seceded before the border South.[3] But there are problems with such simple mathematics. First of all, if those same tables showed the number, rather than the percentage, of slaves, the pattern would change. In 1860, Virginia held more enslaved people than any other Southern state. The border South was fully invested in slavery. Second, suggesting that a delay in secession implied a lack of commitment to slavery ignores the geopolitical calculation that shaped the course of secession.

Unionists in the border South did not waver on slavery; they counseled, in fact, that union offered the best protection for slavery. They were correct.

Moreover, even in the deep South white Southern self-interest in slavery, so real and so obvious, did not lead to one political stance. Many of the largest slaveholders of Mississippi and Louisiana did everything they could to keep their counties and states in the Union. Despite the misleading impressions created by statewide numbers, we find few statistical links between individual slaveholding and votes on secession. Slaveholders were not necessarily more likely than nonslaveholders to vote for immediate secession.

Slavery held profound meaning for every person who lived within its orbit. Slavery's power stretched all the way to the Mason-Dixon Line, into every facet of life. Yet the force of slavery was refracted through prisms of social practice and belief. Slavery defended itself with Unionism as well as with secession, with delay as well as action. Each county's and state's strategy depended on where it fitted in the machinery of American politics.[4]

Northern politics proved just as complicated as that of the South. Men held political loyalties for reasons that had little to do with slavery. Democrats appealed to Catholics and to men who wanted the government to tax them as little and to do as little as possible. Republicans appealed to Protestants and to men who wanted the government to accelerate economic growth and expansion. Slavery presented itself to many Republicans as an obstacle to Northern progress. White Northerners strongly opposed to slavery often viewed the Republicans with mistrust.

Predicting which men in a county or state would vote for the new Republican party proved challenging in 1860 and is difficult even in retrospect. The gears of the Northern political mechanism spun around many axes, of which slavery was only one—and not always the most important one.

The political mechanisms of the North, the South, and the nation as a whole had to be reset several times in the late 1850s and early 1860s. The regular rhythms of the 1840s, when victories between the Democrats and Whigs swung back and forth in small and predictable arcs, gave way to erratic and jolting swings. The Whigs died, the Know-Nothings came and went, and the Republicans emerged. Powerful and unforeseeable events jarred the regular patterns of elections. John Brown's raid and the Dred Scott decision, Lincoln's election and the secession conventions made the old political mechanism seem obsolete, unable to keep up with the pace of events. The political meaning of slavery changed with each occurrence, shifting with events, reactions to events, and reactions to the reactions.

The political system itself helped bring on the Civil War. The mechanism assembled over the first half of the nineteenth century turned around binary choices between two parties and only two parties. Party regulars demanded that true loyalists were all or nothing. To be undecided and open to persuasion was to be less than a man. As the two-party system strained and broke in the 1850s, American voters took this habit of mind with them; they felt driven to dichotomous choices of Republican or Democrat, Union or Confederacy. Voices of caution and moderation were drowned out beneath charges of cowardice and betrayal. With each decision the next round of choices became even narrower: yes or no, now or never, with us or against us.

Slavery drove the United States to the Civil War, as the fundamentalists argue, but politics determined the momentum, timing, and outcome of regional suspicion and hostility, as the revisionists insist. We can reconcile the truth of the fundamentalists with the truth of the revisionists by focusing on the connection between structure and event, on the relationships between the long-existing problem of slavery and the immediate world of politics. The Civil War was caused neither by the mere existence of slavery nor by the twists and turns of politics, however, but rather by catalysts that emerged in the two or three decades before the war began.

To understand these catalysts we need to set aside a formula that has come to seem obviously true: The war as a conflict between a modern North and a pre- or antimodern South.[5] In this kind of fundamentalist interpretation, everything fits together neatly. Economy, politics, religion, gender relations, literacy, demography—everything aligns along the opposing axes of modernity on either side of the Mason-Dixon Line. This interpretation avoids granting the North an enlightened racial vision but grants it instead the sanction of world history. The North could not help fighting for autonomy, technology, diversity, and progress, for that is what modernity demands. The South could not help fighting for hierarchy, agriculture, homogeneity, and the past, for that is what modernity has overcome. Exactly why differing degrees of modernization needed to lead to war is left unexplained, but it apparently seems self-evident to many people.

The role of modernity in the Civil War might better be understood as a catalyst for both the North and the South rather than as a simple difference between them. The debate and anger that fed into what became the Civil War contained "modern" elements that would not have existed before the middle of the nineteenth century: a struggle over a hypothetical railroad, a novel written by an obscure woman, an act of symbolic terrorism, a media war over a distant territory.

There can be little doubt that the North embodied many elements of what we would now see as modern: high literacy, rapidly growing towns and cities, early and widespread adoption of industrial methods, innovation in transportation and communication, the dominance of market values, and strong political engagement by a broad electorate of white men. The new Republican party combined these various notions in a potent ideology. The slave South generated fewer towns and factories than the North, to be sure, and its lower population density sustained fewer schools and newspapers. On the other hand, the white South welcomed political parties, nationalism, and political mobilization; it welcomed print, rapid change in ideas, and intimate connection to the cultural centers of Europe and the North; it welcomed the adoption of useful machinery of production and transportation, openness to immigration, rapid growth in churches, higher education, and missionary societies.[6]

Make no mistake: Southern slavery was, as W. E. B. DuBois put it, "a cruel, dirty, costly and inexcusable anachronism, which nearly ruined the world's greatest experiment in democracy," a system of oppression that created "widespread ignorance, undeveloped resources, suppressed humanity and unrestrained passions."[7] But the American South created prosperity for much of its white population, a sophisticated means of communication and governance, and a sense among white Southerners of themselves as an advanced and enlighted Christian people. The slave South, in other words, was modern in precisely the ways that encouraged white Southerners to think of themselves as members of a new nation with a destiny all their own, that allowed the Confederacy to form an enormous army out of almost nothing, and that permitted them to wage effective war against the most thoroughly modern state in the world for four years. Slavery was not accidental in this process, not a mere drag on progress, but gave the Confederacy its only reason for existence.

Two critical components of modernity shared by the North and the South—print and popular politics—created the necessary contexts for the war. Print permitted people to cast their imaginations and loyalties beyond the boundaries of their localities, to identify with people they had never met, to see themselves in an abstract cause. People learned to imagine consequences of actions, to live in the future.[8]

Print shaped everything we associate with the coming of the Civil War. Although Bleeding Kansas was far removed from the East and John Brown's raid freed no slaves, these events gained critical significance because they were amplified and distorted by newspapers. Without the papers, many events we now see as decisive would have passed without wide consequence. With the papers, events large and small stirred the American people every day. The press nurtured anticipation and grievance. Americans of the 1850s grew newly self-conscious, deeply aware of who they were and who others said they were. The "North" and the "South" took shape in words before they were unified by armies and shared sacrifice.

It was surely no accident that a long-brewing sectional animosity boiled over when railroads, telegraphs, and newspapers proliferated in the 1840s and 1850s. Suddenly, local bargains and gentlemen's agreements in Washington could not stand. Politicians could no longer get away with saying one thing in one place and something altogether different somewhere else, for their speeches raced ahead of them by telegraph and newspapers. Rival editors wrenched the most inflammatory words out of context, underlining their danger, amplifying their threat. Territorial expansion took on a new meaning when railroads and steamboats accelerated America's frantic rush in every direction, when American Indians were removed and foreign threats faded.

The Civil War was brought on by people imaginatively constructing chains of action and reaction beyond the boundaries of their own time and space. In distinctly modern ways, people North and South in 1860 and 1861 anticipated events, made warnings and threats, imagined their responses, imagined the responses of others. This is one reason the Civil War seems to have, as Lincoln put it, "come," why the war seemed both inevitable and surprising, easily explainable yet somehow incomprehensible. People on both sides were playing out future scenarios even as they responded to immediate threats. They recognized how deeply contingency could run and how quickly things could shift; a Supreme Court decision or a presidential election could change the evolution of vast structures of slavery and economic development.

The political system joined print in teaching Americans to think of themselves as connected to places beyond their communities. Long before an integrated national economy evolved, political parties welded American places together. The Democrats, Whigs, and Republicans gave Americans common cause with people who lived thousands of miles away while dividing them against their neighbors and relatives. The political system existed for such connections, for cooperation and division. The system created policy to help feed the machinery, created controversy to attract the undecided, created positions to reward the faithful. The system was the end as well as the means.[9]

The role of modernity in the American Civil War, in short, was exactly the opposite of what we usually take it to be. A modern North did not go to war to eradicate an antimodern South. Instead, modernity was a shared catalyst between North and South, a shared medium, a necessary precondition for anything like the war that began in 1861.

What caused the Civil War? If you have to offer a one-word answer, go ahead and just say slavery. But you should know what you mean by that answer. The Civil War did not come from the sheer intolerable existence of slavery in a nation built on the ideals of freedom, or from the past and the future caught in a death struggle, or from a familiar sequence of political events that crashed into one another in a chain reaction like so many billiard balls. Rather, you mean slavery as the key catalytic agent in a volatile new mix of democratic politics and accelerated communication, a process chemical in its complexity and subtlety. You mean, in short, history, the living connection among fundamental structures, unfolding processes, and unpredictable events.

In one field of human understanding after another, a cultural historian has recently reminded us, causality has come to be understood in terms of "increasing specificity, multiplicity, complexity, probability, and uncertainty."[10] Historical understanding needs the same perspective, what I have called deep contingency. The perspective argues for the intricate interplay of the structural and the ephemeral, the enduring and the emergent. Simple stories of intrinsic qualities and unfolding inevitability are not worthy of history. We should simply refuse to settle for simple explanations for complex problems.

Deep contingency should be distinguished from what we might call surface contingency, the familiar historical staples of accident, personality, and timing, the clichés of what ifs and almosts. By itself, a recognition of surface contingency leads only to the predictable observation that battles and elections are unpredictable. While surface contingency can sometimes trigger deep contingency, the great majority of unpredictable events come and go without much consequence; deep contingency reverberates throughout the recesses of the social order. To understand deep contingency we must try to comprehend a society as a whole, its soft structures of ideology, culture, and faith as well as its hard structures of economics and politics. All structures must be put into motion and motion put into structures. It is hard, of course, perhaps impossible, to portay deep contingency in a fully satisfactory way, but that should not stop us from trying.

There is no way to understand history except to study it, to question it, to challenge it. History does not fit on a bumper sticker. New evidence, new methods, and new perspectives nec-

essarily change our understanding of history, and we should welcome revisionist history just as we welcome revisionist medicine
and revisionist science. History that comes to us as nostalgia and
fable does more harm than good. Honest history answers our
questions only by asking something of us in return.

EXPORTING

RECONSTRUCTION

For over 100 years now the United States has been the great agent of social transformation in the world. From the Philippines at the beginning of the twentieth century to Iraq at the beginning of the twenty-first, this country has sought to remake other nations. In our highest and most abstract language, we say we want the reconstructed countries to be democratic, open, humane, and under the rule of law. Speaking more concretely, we call for open markets and free elections. Speaking with frank self-interest, we demand friendly regimes, access to crucial resources, and advantage within the harsh realities of global geopolitics.

From the Fourteen Points to the Marshall Plan, from Korea to Afghanistan, the leaders of the United States, whatever their party or ideology, have pursued these reconstructions. Some presidents have worked to rebuild in the wake of fascism, some in opposition to communism, and some to replace failed or hostile regimes. Sometimes, as in Japan and Germany after World War II, the efforts at political and social reconstruction have proved remarkably successful. In other times and places, reconstructions have failed to further the cause of liberal democracy.[1]

In none of these places, ironically, has the United States held up its own Reconstruction as a model. This may seem surprising, for Reconstruction in the South embodied most of the themes of later interventions. It attempted to use coordinated state power to destroy a nondemocratic regime. It deployed military and bureaucratic agents to oversee the transformation. It brought in philanthropic allies to help in the building of schools and other institutions at the boundary of domestic and public life. It counted on the power of markets, contracts, and profits to reinvent the economy.

American policy makers ignore their own Reconstruction for a reason. Despite its dramatic story of social transformation, America's Reconstruction bears an anomalous place in the self-understanding of our country. Our most popular movies and novels have told us for generations that Reconstruction was a horrible mistake, a misguided, hypocritical, and deluded effort by zealots to force an unnatural order on a helpless South. The millions of white Americans who watched *The Birth of a Nation* in 1915 or *Gone with the Wind* in 1939 absorbed this story of Reconstruction. No popular film or novel has told a positive story of the men and women who risked—and gave—their lives to reconstruct the South. The most evocative portrayal of recent decades, Toni Morrison's *Beloved*, views Reconstruction across the haunted distance of the Ohio River and through lenses of unbearable African American sadness and loss. Reconstruction holds remarkable stories of struggle and success, but those stories have yet to find their artist.[2]

American historians, for their part, have offered an array of reasons to explain why Reconstruction failed. The nation's first generation of professional scholars told their readers early in the twentieth century that black people simply were not prepared for freedom, much less for citizenship, that the leaders of Reconstruction in the South were rootless, incompetent, and morally bankrupt Yankees who came to the South only to pillage it. In the generation after World War II, with the occupations of Japan and Germany fresh in people's minds, historians argued that Reconstruction had failed for exactly the opposite reason, that it had not gone nearly far enough in removing former Confederates from power or in providing the freed people the land and justice they deserved.

Only an African American historian, W. E. B. DuBois, saw Reconstruction through the eyes of those it tried to help. He documented the efforts freed people made to secure their own equality and gave due credit to the white Radicals. But DuBois despaired of being heard. By the 1930s, when he wrote, Reconstruction had long settled into a way for white people to use that part of American history "for pleasure and amusement, for inflating their national ego."[3]

In recent decades historians have painted Reconstruction in ever more muted colors. The magisterial 1988 history by Eric Foner, sympathetic to African Americans, their accomplishments, and their allies, nevertheless deemed Reconstruction "America's unfinished revolution."[4] Most historians agree that Reconstruction held possibility and heartening idealism but could not overcome white Southern resistance and Northern ambivalence; its greatest accomplishments were the latent possibilities of the Fourteenth Amendment and black Southern leaders who would not rest until they had redeemed the promise of equality. Other products of Reconstruction, unfortunately, arrived sooner and in more visible ways: a white backlash of lynchings and disfranchisement; a sense of victimization in the white South that was to endure for generations; a Southern resentment of any effort the federal government might exert to ameliorate local injustice. Reconstruction is the Bermuda Triangle of American history, a place where we lose our bearings, where the usual American stories of progress and success simply do not work.

The struggles of Reconstruction foreshadowed elements of American-led reconstructions throughout the world. The story prefigured, in different ways, United States involvement in the Philippines and the Dominican Republic a half century after Reconstruction, in Japan and Germany forty years after that, and in Vietnam and Iraq fifty years later. If we can see the familiar story of America's Reconstruction as an episode with counterparts, parallels, and resonances elsewhere, we might be able to make better use of this piece of our national history as we navigate our own times and we might understand our own Reconstruction a bit better. Reconstruction was not an anomaly, a feverish dream, but a precursor to much of American foreign policy around the world in the century since Reconstruction's end.

America's Reconstruction was remarkably complex, varying sharply from one place to another in the South and from one year to the next. It involved the interlocking stories of three major groups: white Northerners, white Southerners, and black Southerners, all in conflict not only with one another but internally as well. As events turned, they tested different alignments and patterns, different alliances and conflicts. The white North wanted irreconcilable goals: vengeance and reconciliation, transformation and stability, justice and the status quo. In the white South many called for peace and acceptance of the new order while others demanded relentless resistance to alien invaders. The black South saw conflicts between former slaves and former free blacks, between people from town and people from the country, between women and men, between secular leaders and religious leaders.

America's Reconstruction was up against long odds from the outset. It sought to complete one of the great revolutions of modern history and to do so without the benefit of overwhelming military force, modern tools of surveillance, or a contrite opponent. Slavery in the United States had been strong and growing stronger when it suddenly ended in a vast war waged over much of the continent. Southern slaveowners held the largest slave population in the hemisphere, an empire that had grown through a massive domestic slave trade and a war with Mexico that determined the future of much of North America. Measured by railroad mileage, telegraphs, white literacy, and political participation, the slave South had uniquely combined the machinery of modernity with enslaved labor. Southerners had dominated the presidency and the Supreme Court throughout the first three generations of United States history, and they did not hesitate to use that power to suppress abolition, to force Northern complicity in returning fugitive slaves, and to lay legal claim to at least half of the nation's territory.[5]

The Republicans dedicated themselves to breaking the hold of what they called the Slave Power Conspiracy, an unholy alliance of officials at the highest level of the federal government. Republicans believed that most white Southerners were Unionists at heart but had become trapped under the power, delusion, and allure of a radical slaveocracy. Given a political alternative, the Republicans thought, Southern nonslaveholders would join their allies outside the South and would lead a slow, quiet, and peaceful internal revolution that would contain the spread of slavery and eventually, generations later, bring the institution to end. They were astonished when eleven slave states, all the way up to Virginia, mobilized for war in the wake of the election of 1860.

Abraham Lincoln hoped, deep into the war that followed his election, that the true Unionist population in the white South would come to its senses. But white Southerners instead became ever more wedded to the cause for which they were dying. The war created the Confederacy, and the Confederacy created The South. As the war dragged on and turned into a fight against slavery, some Republicans called for quick reconciliation with Southern whites and the granting of minimal rights for former slaves. Others called for something more: the provision of political participation for black men they considered especially intelligent and loyal. Others, proud to embrace the label of Radical, called for the transformation of the South, for the destruction of the slaveholder class, for the elevation of former slaves into full citizens, for the provision of land to the people who had worked it without compensation for generations. They wanted Reconstruction to be a revolution.

Frederick Douglass, as he so often did, went to the heart of the matter. The question before the United States in 1866 was "whether the tremendous war so heroically fought and so victoriously ended shall pass into history a miserable failure, barren of permanent results—a scandalous and shocking waste of blood and treasure . . . of no value to liberty or civilization."[6] The Civil War by itself had left almost all the hard questions about the nation's future unsettled. As Douglass saw, Reconstruction would be a race between the forces of change loosed by the war and the forces of reversion. America's Reconstruction, like all those that would follow, saw a desperate competition between the spread of democracy and a desire for political, economic, and racial stability.

When the war ended, the United States government had no explicit and coherent plan for the postwar South. Lincoln's assassination threw things into even greater uncertainty, and the rise of a Southerner, Andrew Johnson, to the presidency confused things more. White Southerners, unrepentant after their military defeat, treated their conquerors with contempt. They unleashed riots in Memphis and New Orleans, created the Ku Klux Klan, and enacted Black Codes that sought to reinscribe as much slavery as possible in the postwar world. White resistance galvanized the power of the Radicals among the Republicans and brought Radical Reconstruction down on the South in the spring of 1867, two years after the war had ended.

White Southerners won a victory in their counterrevolution when they managed to hang derogatory names on lead characters in Reconstruction: carpetbaggers and scalawags. In neutral language, carpetbaggers were non-Southern Republicans holding office in the South, necessary agents of political leadership and social transformation. Scalawags were white Southern Republicans willing to ally themselves with new African American citizens. In the white Southern lexicon, carpetbaggers were avaricious, small-minded, opportunistic scavengers who descended on the South for profit; they were unprincipled hypocrites who ignored injustice in their own states while elevating ill-prepared slaves into the highest political offices. The scalawags were turncoats to their region and their race, ready to sell their heritage in return for a cheap political office.

For all their vitriol against the carpetbaggers and scalawags, it was really black Southerners that white Southerners feared and despised. In the white Southern portrayal, African Americans simply possessed no capacity for democracy. In reality, black Southerners showed a remarkable ability to understand democratic politics and to use those politics to advance their own ends. They mobilized quickly and effectively, posing a powerful threat in numbers and leadership. "This is a democracy—a government of the people," argued a convention of African Americans in Nashville in January 1865, as they petitioned white Unionists for a voice in the future that stretched before them. "It should aim to make every man, without regard to the color of his skin, the amount of his wealth, or the character of his religious faith, feel personally interested in its welfare. Every man who lives under the Government should feel that it is his property, his treasure, the bulwark and defense of himself and his family, his pearl of great price, which he must preserve, protect, and defend faithfully at all times, on all occasions, in every possible manner." White Southerners feared black people all the more for their eloquence and effectiveness in creating voters from former slaves. Whites resented the positive things Reconstruction governments accomplished, the schools and other institutions they built, the laws and constitutions they democratized.[7]

Most white Southerners never accepted the legitimacy of Reconstruction. They eventually crushed Reconstruction through violence, terrorism, and fraud, through loyalty to the old regime and white supremacy. Some Southern states saw Reconstruction end quietly, in backroom deals among conservative men eager to bring the conflict to a close. Other Southern states saw Reconstruction end in open warfare, as armed white men terrorized black and white Republicans in their homes, in swamps and woods, at church and at the polls. Reconstruction as a whole finally ended in the wake of a confused and corrupt presidential election in which the future of black Americans was used as a bargaining chip.

When Reconstruction was gone, the white majority rejoiced that finally the day of true law, true justice, had returned. The South, they declared, was "redeemed." The white South used every means, legal and illegal, over the next ninety years to contain, roll back, nullify, and deny the transformations initiated by Reconstruction. They waged, and won, a war of propaganda. Woodrow Wilson, president of Princeton and soon to be president of the United States, articulated the understanding of Reconstruction many educated white people held at the beginning of the twentieth century. Reconstruction had seen a vast class of people, once slaves, "unpracticed in liberty, unschooled in self-control; never sobered by the discipline of self-support, never established in any habit of prudence; excited by a freedom they did not understand, exalted by false hopes; bewildered and without leaders, and yet insolent and aggressive; sick of work, covetous of pleasure—a host of dusky children untimely put out of school." Reconstruction failed in America, at heart, because white people could not imagine that black Americans deserved freedom and equality. Moreover, because white Americans denied black Americans what they deserved, white Americans felt obligated to denigrate and abuse black people for generations to come.[8]

For decades after Reconstruction the North ran the federal government largely for its own benefit, stacking the deck against the South in banking, transportation, pensions, and taxes, skimming money from the poorest part of the country and retarding progress for black and white alike. Because white Northerners got everything they needed from the government, they could afford to offer words of sympathy to white Southerners over their "race problem" and could express regret for any "excesses" of Reconstruction. Many whites in the North had serious doubts about what they had caused, about the way their resistance to the Democrats in 1860 had metastasized into widespread emancipation, enfranchisement, and empowerment of former slaves by 1867. White Northern voters, weary of thinking about the "Southern Question," began pulling back from Reconstruction almost the moment they initiated it.

Despite its particularities, the path the South followed after the Civil War bore strong resemblances to that followed by other defeated societies in the late nineteenth and early twentieth centuries. Much like France after its defeat by the Prussians in 1871 and Germany after its defeat in World War I, white Southerners sifted through history until they could construct a plausible and reassuring explanation for why things were as they were. The white South, a grieving survivor of its own history, played out stages of acceptance, rejection, and redefinition of defeat. At first the vanquished lived in a sort of dreamland in which they imagined that all would return to the way it had been before. White Southerners believed in 1865 that they would quickly rejoin the Union and that slavery would endure in fact, if not in name. Former Confederates refused to believe that the North would humiliate their fellow white Americans by reconstructing them or that the victors could do so even if they wanted to.[9]

Such dreams ended with sudden awakening. When the expectations of easy reconciliation turned out to be fantasies and the victor did indeed insist on exploiting his advantage, the loser felt doubly betrayed. The only acceptable explanation for defeat must have been that the winner cheated in some way. In the South, as in Europe, the "cheating" involved the opponent's use of new technologies, propaganda, blockades, or sheer numbers— unchivalric, unmanly ways of conquering a foe superior on the battlefield proper. The losing side considered the war to be sheer greed marching under the banner of some higher excuse. The defeated people understood themselves to be those whom God punished and tested because they best upheld his teaching and example. Defeat became moral purification. The cause for which they had fought was blameless, spotless; the real evil lay with Babylon, with Caesar.

The conquered peoples of the white South, of France in the 1870s, and of Germany in the 1920s spun out myths of virtue in which accounts would eventually be settled. In the South, few spoke after 1865 of the battlefield conquest of the Yankees, no matter how many may have fantasized about such revenge, but rather of winning the battle the Radicals claimed as their ultimate victory: black freedom and equality. If the white South could push back African American advances, it could in a real sense still win the war. That struggle was fought in the guerrilla warfare of the chain gang and the lynch mob; it was fought in statehouses where legal segregation and disfranchisement were inscribed into the law of the land. The men who led the white Southern counterrevolution over Reconstruction, the "Redeemers," claimed to defend the integrity not only of the South but of white people everywhere. They became warriors for their entire race—the proud Aryans, the opening titles in *The Birth of a Nation* called them—fighting once again on the front lines, this time certain to be victorious.[10]

When the United States sought to recast the Philippines and the Dominican Republic near the turn of the century, America's understanding of Reconstruction at the time offered an easy explanation for both the necessity of the interventions and any failure they faced: race. Darker peoples, America's leaders assumed, simply did not possess the genius of democracy and therefore had to be schooled. But only so much could be expected from them; any failures were products of their limitations, not of any American intervention. More promising was Europe, where the devastation after World War I created opportunities for the United States to reconstruct white civilization so that democracy could once again flourish. The carnage and waste of the war did not undermine Woodrow Wilson's faith that the unique talents of Europeans would permit them to rebuild democracy with America's aid.

The failure of the United States to join the League of Nations, however, signaled that many Americans had no taste for reconstruction anywhere. Disdain for the South's Reconstruction flourished during the isolationist years of the 1920s and 1930s. Claude Bowers's full-throated attack on Reconstruction, *The Tragic Era*, became a best seller in 1929, and Charles and Mary Beard's enormously influential *Rise of American Civilization*, published in multiple editions in the 1930s, portrayed Reconstruction as a crucial and cynical stage in the takeover of the United States by industrial capitalism. *Gone with the Wind* translated this common perception of Reconstruction into compelling fictional form in 1936, and the movie based on the book was a national sensation in 1939.

Victory in World War II changed that trajectory. Suddenly the United States found itself once again an occupying power, this time in the unlikely location of Japan. This reconstruction proved more satisfying for the American people. In the wake of unimaginable loss, the Japanese lay completely at the mercy of the occupying Americans. Japanese soldiers returned home in disgrace, and the Japanese people denounced leaders of the old regime. General Douglas MacArthur ruled the defeated nation with wide-ranging authority. In Japan the defeated people "embraced defeat," accepting much of their opponent's assessment of their failings and taking much of what the United States offered.

Japan's transformation unfolded as all victors wish reconstructions would unfold, but even Japan's reconstruction turned out to be less ideal than Americans often remember. After three years of reconstruction the Japanese became restless under American stewardship. The embrace grew chilly, the resentment more obvious; by 1949 a majority of Japanese told pollsters they thought their country was headed in the wrong direction. The Japanese made *Gone with the Wind* a best-selling novel that year, imagining themselves in the place of Scarlett O'Hara, living in a strange new world led by outsiders. They could imagine another day, a day when they would guide their own history.[11]

Despite the shared appeal of *Gone with the Wind*, the reconstruction of Japan and the reconstruction of the American South appeared to have little in common. Compared with Japan, the object of relentless bombing raids, including the first use of atomic weapons, the American South emerged from the Civil War relatively intact. Its infrastructure, far more rural than that of Japan, was quickly rebuilt. The Union army melted away quickly in the South after Appomattox, leaving a weak military force to check former Confederates who would control the South. Confederate soldiers were lionized, not humiliated. The Confederacy, far from being discredited, was held up as the embodiment of virtue and sacrifice. A culture of defiance rather than defeat marked the white South.

The pattern of the South has proved to be more typical in other reconstructions than the pattern of Japan. In fact, our own

Reconstruction may be more useful as a guide to what to expect elsewhere in the world than any other reconstruction in which the United States has engaged. The size and complex geography of the South, the prominent role of race, the armed strength of an unrepentant foe, the appeal to religion, the ability of opponents to control local loyalties and structures of power, and the popular appeal of narratives of opposition to overwhelming outside force make America's Reconstruction an all too fitting test bed for other reconstructions the nation might undertake. Americans might take a number of lessons from our own history as we look out upon a world we are tempted to remake.[12]

Reconstructions, first of all, tend to follow wars and partake of all the dislocation, confusion, and corruption of war, inevitably finding war's burdens a heavy load to carry. Defeated people's memories collapse the suffering of war into the suffering of the reconstruction that follows. White Southerners have long conflated Sherman's march with an imagined devastation that Reconstruction, among the mildest of military occupations, did not in fact bring. They have confused black freedom with permanent economic devastation and blamed the Yankees for generations of Southern poverty and injustice.

Second, reconstruction often creates among the reconstructed people a coherence, identity, and solidarity they did not possess before. Rooting out problems creates new problems, new opponents, new combinations, and new identities. In the South, Reconstruction rather than the Civil War became the true object of contempt and hatred by postwar whites, the object of self-righteousness and retribution. Reconstruction displaced the guilt white Southerners may have felt for secession, the shame they may have felt in losing the Civil War. Reconstruction rather than slavery became defined as the cardinal sin of the era.

Third, reconstructions foster steadfast and violent defenders of the old order. A quest for purity, for return, for the respect of the fallen fathers animates counterreconstructions. When things go wrong, the opponents of reconstruction can always claim that things were better under the old regime and find some who agree. Former Confederates became heroes in the postwar South, their reputations actually burnished by Reconstruction if they remained true to the Lost Cause. The only Confederates to fall into disgrace were those, such as James Longstreet, who joined the Republicans. The "Old South," an imagined land of gentility and paternalism, was perfected by the New South for its own purposes.

Fourth, reconstructions demand a disruption of the standing economic order yet bring an immediate need for the cooperation of those who prospered most in the old order. Powerful families tend to remain powerful families. The leaders of reconstructions often make deals with unsavory people when success comes to seem more important than purity.

Fifth, economic reconstruction is an unavoidable part of any social reconstruction, but quarantining greed and the appearance of greed is hard. Reconstructor nations can easily seem to be carpetbagger nations. The white South, for its part, used every instance of Northern self-interest as proof that all of Reconstruction was a false front, a mere ploy to advance Yankee greed. Several generations of historians fed this story, portraying Reconstruction as a capitalist strategy to install industrial power in the federal government. Even today many people still hold to this unsubstantiated notion and read the Civil War backward to see the entire sectional struggle as a cynical fight over tariffs or tax policy.

Sixth, in order to be reconstructed, people need to be perceived as needing to be reconstructed. Accordingly, they are often attributed with pathologies, ingrained limitations, and flawed heritages. Conflicts of interest and power tend to be imagined as problems of race, religion, or civilization. When the objects of reconstruction refuse to be thoroughly reconstructed, they appear incapable or unworthy of being reconstructed. White Southerners have long labored under images of recalcitrance, bloodthirstiness, and backwardness forged in Reconstruction. Black Southerners, thanks to the efforts of their political opponents, have long been portrayed as hapless political actors, foolish in their ambition and corrupt in their attempts to accomplish that ambition.

Seventh, the clock is always ticking. Reconstructions are a race between change and reaction; they cannot last long before they seem another form of oppression. Because they are hard for both the occupying force and the place they occupy, reconstructions must make their changes quickly or they are not likely to make them at all even though the deep change implied by the very word "reconstruction" inevitably takes a long time to instill. In the American example, Andrew Johnson wasted the immediate postwar era in which the South was most pliable. By the time the Radicals took over the resistance had become entrenched, rearmed, confident, and determined.

Eighth, reconstructions often go further and in different directions from those which their creators intended. Reconstructions unleash irreconcilable goals and aspirations among different actors, differences buried, obscured, and mediated during normal times. Black Americans proved to be hungrier and better prepared for full participation in politics than even many Radicals expected. Advocates for women's rights seized upon Reconstruction to demand that the movement for inclusion and full citizenship apply to females throughout the United States. Labor unions in the North marched under the same ideals of equality and freedom the Republicans promoted in the South. American Indians rose in rebellion against the forces of the United States during the years of Reconstruction, demanding self-determination. Reconstructions tend to become revolutions, and revolutions are hard to manage.

Ninth, freedom is a mercurial ideal. Those involved in Reconstruction spoke of freedom, but they all meant different things by that word. The Northern white advocates of freedom meant freedom for former slaves to make their livings by the sweat of their own brows. The black advocates of freedom meant freedom to build independent lives for them and their families. The opponents of Reconstruction appealed to home rule, self-determination, defense of the hearth. All these were American words, American ideals, but they could not be reconciled in the South of the 1860s and 1870s.

Finally, and perhaps most important, reconstructions can fall victim to their own ideals. The Radical Republicans demanded so much of their Reconstruction that it could not help failing even by its own standards. Flush with military victory, furious with the Rebels who had taken so many white Northerners down with them, appalled at the conditions of slavery they saw firsthand in the defeated South, the Radical Republicans announced that they would settle for nothing less than the utter transformation of the South. They proclaimed that if their plans came to pass in the South, "the wilderness shall vanish, the church and school-house will appear . . . the whole land will revive under the magic touch of free labor."[13]

Conflating every dream of social reconstitution—prosperity, justice, and equality—was dangerous enough by itself. But when economic self-interest on the part of the conquerors combined with cultural arrogance toward black and white Southerners alike, the entire edifice of Reconstruction threatened to topple of its own weight. Republicans ignored the segregation and disfranchisement of African Americans that marred most Northern states, demanding a standard for the South they refused to apply to themselves. White Southerners hammered away relentlessly on this inconsistency of their would-be reconstructors, claiming that it nullified the moral standing of the white North.

Republicans portrayed themselves not only as agents of democracy but as agents of economic transformation. They would remake the South along Northern lines, with shrewd and far-sighted investments in railroads, levees, and roads. They bragged that their Yankee business acumen would make the South prosper in a way it had never prospered under the leadership of the lazy and incompetent slaveholder regime. When railroad financing collapsed in the panic of 1873 and states defaulted in their payments, accordingly, the entire Republican regime suffered damage. The Republicans suddenly appeared as bumbling and corrupt incompetents rather than as astute modernizers. Every instance of bribery or malfeasance in one Southern state, moreover, was held up by white Southerners as an example of the moral bankruptcy of all Republicans everywhere. By talking of social progress as one seamless object of democracy, capitalism, probity, and disinterested virtue, the Republicans put every part of their agenda at risk.[14]

The righteous invocation of justice, history, and progress on behalf of a purpose that is also a struggle for power is dangerous. It can create a self-righteous terror in opposition that believes itself to be on the side of God, of race, and of history. Conflict can be escalated morally as well as militarily. It was no accident that the Ku Klux Klan clothed itself in the garb of militant Christianity. The claim of the moral high ground by the opponents of black freedom and equality may have done more damage to the United States in the long run than the political and economic failures of the late 1860s and early 1870s. For generations, a false memory associated racial progress with a deluded dream, with hypocrisy, greed, corruption, and incompetence. That distorted memory has proved to be Reconstruction's most dangerous legacy.

A hard paradox lies at the heart of all reconstructions: The reconstructor must transform a society in its own image without appearing selfish or self-righteous. Our nation tends to wrap its actions in the highest language of freedom, in universal appeals to timeless ideals, but to outside observers those words seem a flimsy covering for mere aggrandizement and global positioning. In the process, the idealistic words are more than tarnished; they are seen as lies. America appears as the thing it least wants to be, a carpetbagger nation.

Ever since Woodrow Wilson white Southerners have been among the most eager in America's efforts to remake the world. Lyndon Johnson, Jimmy Carter, Bill Clinton, and George W. Bush, in widely varying ways, tried reconstruction. Southerners have eagerly voted for presidents of either party who put forward aggressive foreign policy goals. White Southerners declare themselves the most patriotic of Americans. They have been eager to support radical reconstructions elsewhere in the world.

The great Southern historian C. Vann Woodward thought Southerners might bring a different perspective to America's vision of itself. In 1953, when the United States confronted a profoundly dangerous world, Woodward told fellow Southern historians that "with all her terrible power and new responsibilities, combined with her illusions of innocence and her legends of immunity from frustration and defeat, America stands in greater need than she ever did of understanding her own history." Woodward, writing during the intense days of the cold war, worried that people elsewhere anguished over the consequences of America's leadership of the world because in their eyes, the United States had no history to provide gravitas to its judgments. Americans' unwillingness to acknowledge "the tragic and ironic aspects of man's fate," many outside the United States feared, would lead us to unleash social consequences we could neither understand nor control.

Woodward reminded his readers that in fact "America has a history. It is only that the tragic aspects and the ironic implications

of that history have been obscured by the national legend of success and victory and by the perpetuation of infant illusions of
innocence and virtue." It was the South's history, Woodward
argued, that could build a bridge of understanding between
Americans and people in every other part of the world. It was
black and white Southerners who knew different varieties of
defeat, who knew the humiliation, confusion, and frustration that
came from living through Reconstruction and its aftermath. If our
policy makers would pay attention to this part of their nation's
history, they could lead the nation more wisely.[15]

Any effort at reconstruction, our nation's history shows us,
must be implemented not only with determination and might but
also with humility and self-knowledge. Those traits come naturally if we pay due respect to the hardest parts of our own history,
if we allow ourselves to understand that Americans too have
known defeat, loss, and failure on their own soil. In our
Reconstruction, Americans played out all the roles of reconstruction anywhere. We were the agents of revolution and its opponents, its beneficiaries and its victims. Reconstruction, looked at
in the full light of history, offers one of our best opportunities to
see ourselves more clearly.

TELLING THE STORY OF

THE NEW SOUTH

A S I DID research on lynching for my first book, I kept seeing discordant images in the microfilmed newspapers. On the very pages where brutal murders were chronicled in terrible detail, cheerful articles about football games and Coca-Cola and the latest best sellers and revival meetings also appeared. I decided to see if I could write a history that included everything on those pages—politics, religion, music, economic life, literature, popular culture, and daily life—that embraced many kinds of Southerners, that dealt with a range of life and emotion in the "New South," the South that had gathered itself after the end of Reconstruction.

With a small fellowship, I drove twelve thousand miles in a four-hundred-dollar car, a vast 1974 Plymouth Satellite with a butterscotch-colored vinyl roof and a bashed-in side I crudely covered with Bondo and a can of spray paint. I moved from one Motel 6 to another as I covered the Southern archives, reading everything I could find about the South during the Gilded Age. As I did so, I thought about the brilliant nonfiction writers who had covered some of the same ground: W. J. Cash, James Agee, and C. Vann Woodward. Had they left anything for me to say?

W. J. Cash's *The Mind of the South*, probably the best-known analysis of the South in the twentieth century, published in 1941, tried to explain why the white Southerners Cash knew in the 1920s and 1930s behaved the way they did. He wanted to explain why mill workers stood with the mill owners when they had every reason to strike, why politicians vacillated between doing nothing and doing wrong, why the middle class remained inert, why religious intolerance and the Ku Klux Klan held the loyalty of so many white people. [1]

We have to allow Cash his own language, for paraphrase fails: "The cotton-mill worker was a pretty distinct physical type in the South; a type in some respects perhaps inferior to even that of the old poor white, which in general had been his to begin with. A dead-white skin, a sunken chest, and stooping shoulders were the earmarks of the breed. Chinless faces, microcephalic foreheads, rabbit teeth, goggling dead-fish eyes, rickety limbs, and stunted bodies abounded—over and beyond the limit of their prevalence in the countryside. The women were characteristically stringy-haired and limp of breast at twenty, and shrunken hags at thirty or forty." The mill town became like a plantation. The mill baron "knew these workmen familiarly as Bill and Sam and George and Dick, or as Lil and Sal and Jane and Lucy." [2]

Cash dutifully, if somewhat reluctantly, cataloged the changes that came to the post-Reconstruction South. He named the cities, counted the towns, enumerated the mills, nodded toward the middle class, appreciated the schools, regretted the increasing prominence of preachers, noticed the spread of a frank language of acquisition and profit, recognized the rise of parvenus, denoted the widespread "insecurity in rank," tallied the philanthropy, detailed the reformers' efforts. Yet he insisted that all the apparent change only strengthened the "Southern pattern," that "simplicity and that pervasive unreality which has always been associated with their simplicity." Cash found little cynicism among these Southerners, no hypocrisy; rather, a "curious innocence." He saw the New South, from the late nineteenth century on, mired in cultural inertia, dysfunction, falsity, myopia. Strong stuff, and for fifty years hundreds of thousands of readers have listened, responding to the grain of truth in *The Mind of the South* and admiring the rhetoric deployed with such skill and vehemence. [3]

Perhaps Cash felt entitled to his mind reading of the South. He had, after all, put in hours in steamy cotton mills during his college summers; he had watched his parents suffer in the Depression; he had worn cardboard in his shoes; he had written his book in a freezing room lit by a single light bulb while neighborhood boys tossed gravel at the window, mocking this strange man who sponged off his parents well into his thirties. Maybe his words grew out of pain and empathy.

The problem is that his words don't sound like it. Cash did not voice the sympathy for the oppressed that has marked, in varying degrees, virtually every book of the New South history published since World War II. Fortunately for Cash's reputation today, he was also contemptuous of the South's planters, businessmen, and politicians, fair game throughout the intervening half century and into the foreseeable future. Yet by today's standards, Cash would have to be considered racist, sexist, and elitist.

Cash turned to psychology to show why poorer whites followed the leaders of the South even when there was no good reason for them to do so, as was almost always. The common white man, he wrote, "identified his ego with the thing called the South as to become, so to say, a perambulating South in little." It simply felt good, Cash thought, for the common man, poor and defeated, to meld his identity with those of his superiors. Cash built from this individual consciousness out, filling the South with the projection of what he imagined to be the psychological traits of the man at the center. As a result, his South was drenched with violence, fantasy, escapism, irrationality. His South had a dreamlike, nightmarish quality to it; the sense of proportion and time are those of sleep, not of sociology. Cash's mind of the South was a gland, secreting uncontrollable substances. His leading men were as lost as his followers.

Whatever else we might say about Cash's book, the pain he felt for the South came through in every word. *The Mind of the South* was a book of passion. As such, it was one of many written between 1929 and 1941. In those bleak years, after decades of segregation and disfranchisement, after the ravages of the Great Depression, sensitive writers could feel the change in the Southern air. Some wrote to hasten the change, others to slow it, others to salvage what they could of the old. The Nashville Agrarians espoused the glories of the South's rural civilization. William Alexander Percy wrote an elegant conservative apologia for the life of a delta planter. Douglas Southall Freeman won national success by composing tributes to Robert E. Lee. Margaret Mitchell's triumph revealed that Cash's acerbic view was very much a minority view of the white South even in the North and abroad. The 1930s marked too a golden age for sociologists and anthropologists studying the South.

In the year of *The Mind of the South* (and Cash's suicide, as it turned out), 1941, James Agee brought anguish to the act of writing about people such as poor Southerners. "It seems to me curious, not to say obscene and thoroughly terrifying," Agee admitted at the beginning of his book on Alabama sharecroppers, *Let Us Now Praise Famous Men,* "to pry intimately into the lives of an undefended and appallingly damaged group of human beings, an ignorant and helplessly rural family, for the purpose of parading the nakedness, disadvantage and humiliation of these lives before another group of human beings, in the name of science, of 'honest journalism' (whatever that paradox may mean), of humanity, of social fearlessness, for money, and for a reputation for crusading and unbias which, when skillfully enough qualified, is exchangeable at any bank for money." Like Cash's, Agee's prose twisted and contorted under the pressure of his doubt. The words surged and swayed, doubled back on themselves, questioned their own sweeping assertions.[4]

C. Vann Woodward spoke in a more confident voice. By 1941 he had already published his first book, *Tom Watson: Agrarian Rebel,* a brilliant portrayal of a famous Southern demagogue. Woodward wrote history for the navy during World War II and then began his masterpiece, *Origins of the New South,* published in 1951. With that

book and its successor, *The Strange Career of Jim Crow*, written in
the midst of the early struggle for legal rights for black
Southerners and published in 1955, Woodward became the leading historian of the South. He maintained that position until his
death almost a half century later.[5]

Woodward took a position directly opposite that of W. J.
Cash. Where Cash evoked the long continuities of Southern culture, Woodward insisted on the sharp breaks in the Southern
past. Where Cash emphasized psychology, Woodward emphasized the hard structures of economy and politics. Despite their
differences, Cash and Woodward shared several assumptions
that they have passed on to us. The two came of age in the inter-
war era, in which "realism" of one sort or another was the goal.
Both H. L. Mencken, Cash's inspiration, and Charles Beard,
Woodward's inspiration, professed to see through history to its
essence underneath. For Mencken, that essence was often
the common man's gullibility; for Beard, it was economic.
Menckenism tended to glorify the man in the know, whether he
was an aristocrat, the educated person conversant with Darwin
or Freud, or the author and readers of *The Mind of the South*.
Menckenism exaggerated that man's wisdom and caricatured
the average American's perceptions. Woodward's Beardianism,
on the other hand, had a more democratic bent. For Woodward,
all men had economic interests that encouraged them to behave
rationally. The common man, black as well as white, knew what
he needed and wanted, though powerful people had their hands
on the machinery of power. The hidden aspect of Woodward's
argument came in the political realm, where corrupt bargains

and smoky room deals tended to count more than public campaigns.

As Woodward recalled about writing *Origins of the New South*, "my interest was in discovering the character, identification, motives, and alliances of the leaders of the new order in the South." He wrote to peel away the layers of illusion—of legend, myth, deception, self-deception, bombast, wishful thinking, stereotype, and foolishness—to get at the reality underneath. For him, that reality was the social, racial, and economic privilege created in the sordid Gilded Age and perpetuated in the decades afterward.[6]

Woodward's focus on political leaders gives his story of the New South a narrative arc of status quo, challenge, and resolution that fits our expectations of a good story. The writing is beautiful, the arguments are subtle, the qualifications carefully placed, but the basic explanation is that certain identifiable people called the shots, directed the society where they wanted it to go. The haves and have-nots were in struggle, with the rich white men who, as Woodward put it, "pretty much ran things" on the one hand and those "who were run, who were managed, and maneuvered and pushed around" on the other. It is in part the clarity of that struggle that makes the book so appealing, that gives the reader the sense of seeing through the Redeemers, of identifying with the oppressed. [7]

As I traveled throughout the South and then as I read hundreds of newspapers, diaries, memoirs, and travel accounts of the New South, I came to realize that Woodward's perspective would not be mine. We were of different generations, backgrounds, temperaments; I had questions and passions that were not his. People indeed assumed that any new history of the New South would necessarily be a revisionist attack on *Origins of the New South*. But despite our differences and despite my hope for an original vision, my approach to Woodward's book could not be straightforward repudiation. The more I read Woodward's book, the more I came to see it as a model of the historian's craft. The book I was writing, so different from his in many ways, emulated that book's style and structure.

Origins' chapters interlock at several levels, including those of language, metaphor, and mood, making Woodward's narrative powerful and resistant to scholarly displacement. It has no introduction and no conclusion; it defines itself not against any one historian but against an ingrained way of seeing the South; it often seems to work by indirection, aside, and allusion. William B. Hesseltine, reviewing Woodward's book in the *American Historical Review* in 1952, praised *Origins* for "wisely" refraining "from attempting to impose a nonexistent unity" upon the New South. An overview of the New South, Hesseltine argued, would not, could not supply a "clearly defined synthesis" because the New South was simply not "a coherent, unified period of southern history." [8]

I found this aspect of Woodward's book extraordinarily appealing. More overt and obvious ways of writing history seemed to foreclose opportunities that Woodward's style did not, seemed to age in ways that his did not. Even as the note cards piled up and more specific kinds of arguments began to form, I continually looked for theories and examples that would let me capture some of the flexibility of Woodward's narrative. Slowly I developed a way I wanted to tell the story. That style was designed to embrace as many people and kinds of activity as possible, to convey a sense of contingency and possibility even within powerful structures.

In Woodward's account, the major changes in public life—segregation and disfranchisement—were largely partisan phenomena, the products of political manipulation imposed by well-placed leaders; in my book, they would appear as social phenomena, systemic and deeply rooted, that politicians tried to harness and contain. For Woodward, segregation was mainly the result of displaced white frustration, a backlash. For me, statewide segregation was not that at all, but rather a halting and uncoordinated reaction to a series of deep changes in transportation, gender roles, and black class structure. I argued that disfranchisement had far less to do with the overt Populist challenge to the Redeemers than it did with black population movement, generational conflict, the growth of towns and cities, and the winner-take-all politics of the American Gilded Age.

I would try to show how social progress or human kindness did not depend on the decisions of the undependable men at the top. People of every walk of life in the South had their own struggles with poverty, injustice, and prejudice that had nothing to do with the Redeemers. A society has many pressure points, many places where people can make a difference. I did not think that the New South would have been a fundamentally different society if only the Populists had won—the promise that drives Woodward's narrative—because the challenges rural Southerners confronted went much deeper than the political or even the credit system.

My book, which appeared as *The Promise of the New South: Life after Reconstruction* (1992), did well and received some attention.

But it stirred some people up. A reviewer in the leading journal in Southern history wrote a long essay accusing me of "settling for" literary criticism's much-denounced "deconstruction." Casually noting that "no one really agrees on what the term means" anyway, this reviewer declared my book "poststructural." He likened my approach to "New Age channeling" and put words such as "reality," "good," "bad," and "meaning" into quotation marks, imagining that I challenged the validity of such concepts. My narrative squandered respectable research, he concluded, though others might profitably mine it for lectures.[9]

Not surprisingly, I disagreed with this diagnosis. My goals of inclusivity and activity were far from the moral relativism and epistemological nihilism the reviewer meant by "poststructuralism." Indeed, *Promise* never denies our ability to find meanings on which we might profitably agree in the patterns of event and words. If anything, the book is what we might call hyperempiricist, its complexity growing out of many facts and voices, not out of doubt about reality. I tried to make space for material that had not fitted into more conventional narratives, combining everything from number crunching to the exegesis of novels. I found that the sharp edges of people and their ideas kept poking holes through the conceptual bags and boxes into which we had tried to cram them.

One way to describe the idea behind *Promise* is to suggest a distinction between fixed narratives and open narratives. Most works of professional history mix, in various proportions, nineteenth-century styles of storytelling with twentieth-century forms of social science. These fixed narratives tend to be organized in a linear way, either chronologically or in the form of an argument, seeking balance and authority. Though history writing is not as formalized as, say, sociology or political science, historians do rely on introductions, chapter summaries, and conclusions, do expect arguments to be clearly labeled as such, and do ask that works be positioned in relation to other studies. Most works of history are implicitly and explicitly measured against this standard of the fixed narrative, tailored to an audience of students and professors.

Open narratives challenge various parts of that formula. In some open histories the authors let the reader in on the way the argument is being constructed; rather than present history as a self-contained and authoritative argument, these historians openly grapple with problematic sources and presentation. Their narratives suggest that the appearance of coherence and a commanding argument may ultimately be less useful than a reckoning with the limits of our knowledge or understanding. Other open histories ask storytelling and language to do more work. Instead of using the narrative as a means to an analytical end outside the story, these histories attempt to fold the analysis into the story itself. They do not simply relate facts or lay out chronicles. They analyze their topics and make arguments, but not in ways that obviously segregate judgment from storytelling. These open histories may intentionally leave ambiguities unresolved or seek tension and resolution less in professional debate than in evidence, characters, and situations.[10]

Most of our books of course range along a continuum somewhere between fixed and open narratives. There is no need to

178 WHAT CAUSED THE CIVIL WAR?

force books into one camp or another. It is impossible to write a perfectly fixed narrative; slippery language and evidence see to that. It is equally impossible to write a perfectly open narrative, for we write and read books precisely to find coherence of some kind. Different tasks call for different kinds of narratives. Anyone who opens an encyclopedia or dictionary does not want to find contingency and uncertainty; someone who wants a broadly inclusive portrayal of a time or place may expect to find pieces that do not fit together snugly.

Promise's overarching theme is that the currents of industrial capitalism, the national state, and new cultural styles ran deeply throughout the New South—far more deeply than Woodward suggested. Those currents created, directly and indirectly, a complex series of backlashes, countercurrents, unexpected outcomes, and archaicisms. As a result, there were things going on simultaneously in the New South that appeared to have little to do with one another but that in fact sprang from a common source, the conflict between the economic, ideological, and cultural legacies of the slave South and those conveyed by the human and material carriers of late nineteenth-century modernity. The personal and public struggles involved in that multifarious conflict were more complicated than any of the categories historians have devised to explain them. (I later used the term "deep contingency" to describe this vision of historical change, but I relied on it before I had a name for it.)

Many kinds of power operated in the New South, and they were not seamless and congruent. The planters ran their plantations but were neglected by the town-based politicians; politicians ran the statehouse but were sneered at by the railroad companies; preachers guided large congregations but were detested by many profane people; women supervised their households but could always be overruled by their husbands; rural merchants held their customers' futures in their hands but saw their own futures controlled by town-based wholesalers; white people assumed themselves superior to the blacks among whom they lived, but blacks laughed at white pretension. *Promise* is about all these various kinds of power, some that operated by coercion, some that operated by persuasion. It multiplies power, puts various kinds of power in competition with others.

Because it tells this morally complicated story, the narrative of *Promise* is built around contained tension, one signaled by the ambiguous and ironic title of the book. I might, it is true, have been able to boil the tensions down to a series of generalizations, but generalizations numb us to the very things the book is after: the emotional shadings of historical experience, the subtle and shifting contexts in which people had to make choices, the contradictory effects of the decisions people did make, the instability of even the most apparently permanent structures. *Promise* tried to evoke the New South by evoking the hard choices its people had to make, every day and in every facet of life, whether they wanted to or not. I intended a consonance between subject and style.

Some of my most insightful reviewers wondered if the open and empathetic approach of *Promise* can help those who are concerned with "the continuing reality of poverty, racial hatred, and profound ignorance" of our region.[11] In the eyes of such readers Woodward offers something I do not, an explanation that seems to be politically useful in a way mine is not. I understand why people say this: I do not offer clear blame or alternatives. *Promise* is not a focused, crusading book in the way that *Origins* and *The Strange Career of Jim Crow* were, though I often wished it could be. There are still plenty of Southern politicians who deserve all the ridicule and anger that can be directed against them, still plenty of irresponsible corporations, still plenty of shallow boosters ready to give away their communities to anyone willing to put up a factory or chain store. Bitter histories of such people have been written, and written well, and we still need to put those people in perspective.

But there are other stories that need telling too, stories with their own political meaning. It is dangerous to let Southern poverty and oppression be the entire story of the South. Told often enough, exclusively enough, such stories unintentionally flatten Southerners, black and white, into stock figures, into simple victims and villains. These stories have become common fare on television and in movies; they crowd out other possible stories, choking our understanding of the human richness created in Southern history. A history book may tell horrendous stories of race and class domination, but jaded readers, young readers, will nod and turn the page. They have heard it all before.

The South has become a formula. The South and its people get to play only limited roles in the story of America; they are dragged into the textbooks and movie houses to demonstrate slavery, to cause the Civil War, to suffer in poverty, to inflict, and partially to overcome, injustice. The result is a South that is easily pegged, easily caricatured, easily explained. That is an injustice, I came to believe, that a history book might actually do something, however small, to counter. *Promise*, in that sense, was meant to be politically engaged, even if I saw little use in discovering once more that Southern planters, mill owners, and politicians were often unjust. Woodward made that point powerfully forty years ago, when he felt it needed to be impressed upon a readership lulled by Southern boosterism and self-congratulation. What we needed when I wrote my book, I thought, were new ways, perhaps less familiar and direct ways, to let people reading about the South for the first time feel the shock and surprise of how deep the injustice ran and how many people struggled in so many ways with and against that injustice.

Promise was written in what I take to be the spirit of Reinhold Niebuhr, the inspiration for the "irony" in Woodward's famous series of essays that came after *Origins*. Niebuhr argued that all people are capable of both self-awareness and self-deception, are "children of light" and "children of darkness"; moral struggles are located *within* individuals as well as *between* them.[12] I tried to evoke the way people of every sort wrestled with those forces within themselves, not only on the political stage but in their families, in their churches, in their relations with neighbors of another skin color. Rather than merely denounce long-dead politicians and planters, I tried to make readers feel by analogy our own complicity in social processes that are still going on, to strike notes that might resonate with our own lives. We might see ourselves reflected in those middle-class Southerners and Northerners who patronized the poor of both races so easily, who so easily explained injustice as the fault of rednecks and robber barons, who sneered at the music and religion loved by millions, who saw the South as a sort of alternately amusing and terrifying place removed a convenient distance from their own lives.

IN MEMORY OF

C. VANN WOODWARD

I N 1 9 2 8 the Commission on Interracial Cooperation of Atlanta offered three awards—of one hundred, sixty-five, and thirty-five dollars—for "the best papers on the subject of Race Relations, submitted by students of Southern colleges during the present school year." Eighty-two students, about fifty of them women, submitted essays. Three young women swept the prizes. Miss Selese Hunter of Louisiana, at school at Baylor, won the top money for her essay "The Professional Negro Paves the Way for New Era."

Twenty-year-old Vann Woodward's essay did not appear on the list of submissions and did not win a prize. But a copy of his contribution mysteriously appears in the CIC papers on microfilm, along with the three winning essays. Maybe young Woodward's entry came in late; maybe it won honorable mention; maybe a later microfilmer recognized his name and decided to include his paper while discarding those of the other unsuccessful candidates. In any case, there it is.

Woodward's contribution bears an intriguing title, "An Incident from the Career of Judge Lynch." The nine-page essay tells of the Atlanta Riot of 1906, which had shaken the streets right below the CIC's offices twenty-two years earlier. "It was the time of dog-days,"Woodward began, his literary aspirations showing, "the season of bad blood and frequent fevers, against which Negro mammies make charms to hang about the necks of their toddling charges."

Woodward blamed the riot on the leadership of Atlanta, its politicians and editors, who invented charges of black assaults on white women for petty partisan ends, fueling white paranoia. "And so a city walked under a pall of low-hanging fear," he wrote, "a stifling mantle that smothers reason and love."

Woodward's allotted space running out, the young author suddenly stopped and offered his moral, insisting that the riot had grown not from the inherent "bestiality" of human nature but from what he called causal elements: "economic forces, race prejudice, sex, politics, journalism, and the concomitant theories of racial superiority and inferiority." "I tend to accept deterministically," the budding scholar announced, his language straining in the attempt, "the maniacal frenzy of the mindless hoards of striplings and street-scum which were caught like chaff in the cyclonic social winds and flung into the madness of the riot." The rioters were acted upon, in other words, determined, their natural "reason and love" swept into cyclones of social winds by the press and the politicians.

Woodward managed to find a fortunate result of the riot: The violence sobered the dominant men of Atlanta, revealing, he

believed, "the necessity for leading individuals of the race to control a demon which could not be trusted to yellow journalism. It
must come through confidence between thinking individuals."
Woodward agreed with the founders of the CIC that the South
would be saved by enlightened leaders, by an awareness of the
social forces driving the masses, by thinking individuals in control
of the "demon."

C. Vann Woodward learned to write with greater power than
he did when he was twenty, of course, fusing his polarities in elegant counterpoint rather than in obvious (and nonprizewinning)
contradiction. But the elements themselves did not change even
as Woodward became a leading historian of the United States.
They are a major part of his legacy to us.

Woodward always saw two purposes in writing Southern history. One was to trace the roots of the wrong; the other was to
find reason to hope those wrongs could be overcome. Though he
often hid his hope in dark and biting language, at the heart of every
work by C. Vann Woodward beats the hope of redemption, of the
turning of the South *by* the South. He had no faith in the North, its
purposes, or its self-professed desire to reform, improve, and
update the South, whether in abolitionism, Reconstruction, or the
Progressive Era. All his stories are about Southern possibility
denied—but surely denied for only a while longer.

Burden, irony, and hope are, for Woodward, part of the same
view of the world. The intrinsic tension among the three gives his
work its shape; remove any of them, and his portrayal collapses.
Without the burden, there is no history; without the irony, there
is no truth; without the hope, there is no purpose. Analysts have

talked with appreciation of Woodward's burden and irony, but the hope has always been more problematic. It has seemed somehow out of character, somehow unworthy of his gravitas.

In fact, Woodward has been accused of wishful thinking, romanticization, golden ageism, and political projection. Most of the revisions of his work have come in revisions of his hopefulness. No, the South would not have been transformed had only the Populists won, critics have said. No, there was no possibility of avoiding segregation in the 1890s. No, the white South gained no special wisdom from its experience of defeat. "What has the historian to do with hope?" Woodward's brilliant and longtime friend David Potter asked him. The words sometimes haunted him, Woodward admitted.

For Woodward, hope was fragile, turning around lost opportunities and critical moments. The reasonableness and goodwill of the Southern people could be all too easily wasted and twisted by stupid, greedy, and corrupt leaders. His Southern masses, black and white, remained faceless, manipulated by those who pulled the strings. Though racism was not natural and had to be whipped up, unfortunately it always *could* be whipped up when need be. The possibility for catastrophe was always as great as the possibility for progress.

Moreover, it was not clear how Woodward's more democratic South would function even if his hope came to pass. Despite his scoffing at the Agrarians, he held Jeffersonian leanings and could not bring himself to praise an industrial or urban South. He deflated those who trafficked in capitalist dreams of prosperity, but it was never clear how the standard of living in the South could rise without economic growth and external sources of capital. He even tried to turn defeat and the lack of prosperity into a moral asset, but the white South seemed, if anything, more bellicose and jingoistic than whites in parts of the country that knew only success.

Time after time, then, Woodward's hopefulness opened him to criticism. He might have played it safe; few are ever criticized for being too bleak, for expecting too little of the South. Yet in some ways the contemporary South has outstripped some of his most hopeful expectations.

To a degree Woodward could not have imagined when he wrote about the first rumblings of the Bulldozer Revolution, the South has, finally, generated the fastest-growing economy and the fastest-growing population in the nation. The strongest retailer in the country proudly speaks with a Southern accent. The South dominates, for good and ill, national politics and the largest Protestant religious denomination in the country.

Despite the distance it still has to travel, the movement for black equality and black freedom changed the South and the nation irrevocably. The South is no longer solid, no longer colonial, no longer afraid of all change. Black people are now moving to the South, the first such voluntary migration in the history of North America. A black middle class is growing, as is political participation. There are reasons to be hopeful.

Still, hope is less prominent in our scholarship now than in the desperate thirties or the Dixiecrat fifties. Even in the wake of the accomplishments of leaders black and white, female and male, who have created a more just South, many seem cynical about the region and its past. On the one hand, the economic change seems to be running on its own dynamic, heedless of our resistance or guidance. On the other hand, the political change has not gone deep enough or brought enough equality or even generosity of spirit.

What, then, can we still take from Woodward's hope? Maybe his example of activism. By writing of hope and then acting on it, he helped make it come true. We all can't write for the Supreme Court, integrate the Southern Historical Association, or march at Selma, as he did, of course, but opportunities are there. We can help the South see itself more clearly, help explain it to the rest of the country and to the world, help it see possibilities it might not imagine, help it connect its residents to their own history, help it get over fixations that limit its honesty and smother its democracy. The very act of writing Southern history is an act of hope, whether or not we admit it to ourselves and one another.

Maybe too we could shift our angle of vision. Woodward's hope was mainly a hope of close calls. Things would have turned out differently if this election had been won, if this decision had not come down. Such a hope was often fragile. Choices seemed to hinge in just one direction: either/or, win/lose, one side or the other. It often depended on quirks of personality and crises of leadership. Once hope is lost, it is often lost forever.

Maybe we could speak instead of *possibility*. Possibility is widely distributed throughout a society and a culture. It resides, often in latent form, in reservoirs of ideology, faith, power, anger, and memory. Possibility is fluid. Pressure exerted in one place can, and usually does, create consequences in apparently unrelated areas. Actions taken for one reason end up bringing completely unexpected consequences. Secession, launched to cement the power of the largest slaveholding class in the modern world, ended up bringing the sudden death of slavery. Defiance to moderate legal change in relations between blacks and whites in the South brought a radical assault on the entire edifice of segregation.

Possibility, clearly, is Woodwardian in spirit. It is full of irony. It is full of danger. And it is full of hope.

Southern history matters today—maybe more than it did in 1938 or 1951. Southern history is now at center stage in both the region and the nation, with debates over slavery reparations, the Confederate battle flag, images of lynching, and the rest filling the papers and airwaves.

We still need to talk about slavery, about the Civil War, about Reconstruction, about popular culture, about the wars of this century, about the freedom struggle, and about the future. We need to talk to people who do not agree with us. We need to listen as well, avoiding labels and quick dismissals. In those conversations we can point out that things have changed suddenly in the Southern past—for good and bad—and can change suddenly again.

C. Vann Woodward resisted the relentless attempts to reduce the South to central themes, genetic determinism, cultural uniformity, social inertia, or any of the other reductions that tempted then as now. He insisted on the hope, on the possibility, at the heart of the South's history.

He was the last to worship at the feet of the fathers. He lived intensely in his own time, taking the best it offered and fighting the worst. We honor him best by doing the same, for our South needs living history just as his did.

ACKNOWLEDGMENTS

"Pieces of a Southern Autobiography": I wrote a longer version of this essay at the invitation of John Boles, who has edited a collection of autobiographies called *Shapers of Southern History* (Athens: University of Georgia Press, 2004). I thank Mary Ann French for her helpful advice on this essay.

"What We Talk about When We Talk about the South": This essay appeared as one of four in a book I coauthored with Patricia Limerick, Stephen Nissenbaum, and Peter S. Onuf: *All Over the Map: Rethinking American Regions* (Baltimore: Johns Hopkins University Press, 1996).

"A Digital Civil War": This essay is published here for the first time. I thank Anne Rubin and Will Thomas for reading the essay as well as for living much of it with me.

"Where the North Is the South": I wrote an earlier version of this essay at the invitation of Michael O'Brien, who edited a special issue of *Southern Cultures* devoted to international perspectives on the South (Winter 1998).

"Worrying about the Civil War": This essay appeared in a festschrift for David Brion Davis, edited by Karen Halttunen and Lewis Perry: *Moral Problems in American Life: New Perspectives in Cultural History* (Ithaca: Cornell University Press, 1998).

"What Caused the Civil War?": Most of this essay is new, but parts appeared in *Momentous Events in Small Places: The Coming of the Civil War in Two American Communities* (Marquette University Press, 1997), the Frank Klement Lectures at Marquette University. I tried out some of the other ideas in the Carl Becker Lectures at Cornell University in 2002. I am grateful to my hosts at both places for their patience and good advice. I appreciate the advice of Katherine Pierce on subsequent drafts.

Will Thomas and I offer a detailed case study of some of the themes of this essay in our digital article, "The Differences Slavery Made: A Close Analysis of Two American Communities," *American Historical Review* (December 2003), available at http://www.vcdh.virginia.edu/AHR/.

"Exporting Reconstruction": This essay began as a talk before the American Society for Legal History in Washington, D.C., in November 2003 and is published here for the first time. I am grateful to Mary Ann French, Melvyn Leffler, Anne Rubin, and Calvin Schermerhorn for their advice on this essay.

"Telling the Story of the New South": Parts of this essay appeared in "W. J. Cash, the New South, and the Rhetoric of History," in Charles Eagles, ed., *The Mind of the South Fifty Years Later* (University of Mississippi Press, 1992), and in "Narrating the New South," *Journal of Southern History* (August 1995), 555–66.

"In Memory of C. Vann Woodward": I delivered a version of this brief essay at a tribute to C. Vann Woodward at the Southern Historical Association meeting in Louisville, Kentucky, in 2000.

NOTES

WHAT WE TALK ABOUT WHEN WE
TALK ABOUT THE SOUTH

1. Benjamin N. Smith, "Southern Discomfort," *Harvard Crimson* (April 6, 1985), 2. Molly Hatchet was one of the many rock groups that rode a Southern rock wave in the 1970s and 1980s, reveling in Southern accents, country and blues styles, and Confederate flags.

2. Peter Gould and Rodney White, *Mental Maps*, 2nd ed. (Boston: Allen and Unwin, 1986), 53–72.

3. See the findings reported in the influential series of books by John Shelton Reed: *The Enduring South: Subcultural Persistence in Mass Society* (Lexington, Mass.: D. C. Heath, 1972); *One South: An Ethnic Approach to Regional Culture* (Baton Rouge: Louisiana State University Press, 1982); *Southerners: The Social Psychology of Sectionalism* (Chapel Hill: University of North Carolina Press, 1983).

4. Eddy L. Harris, *South of Haunted Dreams: A Ride through Slavery's Old Back Yard* (New York: Simon & Schuster, 1993), 232–33; Ray Allen, "Back Home: Southern Identity and African-American Gospel Quartet Performance," in Wayne Franklin and Michael Steiner, eds., *Mapping American Culture* (Iowa City: University of Iowa Press, 1992), 112–35. This is not the first generation to wrestle with such issues; see Arna Bontemps, "Why I Returned," in Henry Louis Gates, Jr., ed., *Voices in Black and White: Writings on Race in America from Harper's Magazine* (New

York: Franklin Square Press, 1993), 33–45, and Ralph Ellison, *Going to the Territory* (New York: Vintage Books, 1987). As Ellison wrote, "In relation to their Southern background, the cultural history of Negroes in the North reads like the legend of some tragic people out of mythology, a people which aspired to escape from its own unhappy homeland to the apparent peace of a distant mountain; but, in migrating, made some fatal error of judgment and fell into a great chasm of mazelike passages that promise ever to lead to the mountain but end ever against a wall." *Going*, 298–99; also see 89–103.

5. *New York Times*, July 31, 1994, A1; Harris, *South of Haunted Dreams*, 152.
6. "Tennessee," on the compact disc *Three Years Five Months and Two Days in the Life of . . .* by Arrested Development (EMI, 1992), deals eloquently with these issues; for a revealing interview with the lyricist for Arrested Development, see Bill Flanagan, "Black History: Speech Meets Curtis Mayfield," *Musician* (June 1993), 60–67.
7. The pioneering work in this field is David Potter's seminal essay "The Historian's Use of Nationalism and Vice Versa," in *The South and the Sectional Conflict* (Baton Rouge: Louisiana State University Press, 1968), 34–83. For Potter's strictures on Southern difference, see 181–82.
8. For a useful statement of such ideas, fusing anthropology and geography, see Arjun Appadurai, "Putting Hierarchy in Its Place," *Cultural Anthropology* 3 (1988), 36–49. I first encountered the incentive to rethink "natural" boundaries in Richard Handler's *Nationalism and the Politics of Culture in Quebec* (Madison: University of Wisconsin Press, 1988). Of more immediate relevance but also more problematic because of its reductionist focus on a world system is Immanuel Wallerstein, "What Can One Mean by Southern Culture?," in Numan Bartley, ed., *The Evolution of Southern Culture* (Athens: University of Georgia Press, 1988), 1–13. For other relevant and related ideas, also see Benedict Anderson, *Imagined Communities* (London: Verso, 1983); Linda Colley, *Britons: Forging the Nation, 1707–1837* (New Haven: Yale University Press, 1992); Liah Greenfeld, *Nationalism: Five Roads to Modernity* (Cambridge: Harvard University Press, 1992); Jack Temple Kirby, *Media-Made Dixie: The South in the American Imagination* (Baton Rouge: Louisiana State University Press, 1978); Werner Sollors, *Beyond Ethnicity: Consent and Descent in American Culture* (New York: Oxford University Press, 1986); James C. Cobb, "Tomorrow Seems like Yesterday: The South's Future in the Nation and the World," in Joe P. Dunn and Howard L. Preston, eds., *The Future South: A*

Historical Perspective for the Twenty-first Century (Urbana: University of Illinois Press, 1991), 217–38.

My own first book, *Vengeance and Justice: Crime and Punishment in the Nineteenth-Century American South* (New York: Oxford University Press, 1984), seems in retrospect to have been a strong offender in creating the South as "the other," sharply bifurcating Northern from Southern culture. While I still believe in the way I described Southern honor, I would not now paint things in such dichotomous ways.

9. The city fathers of the hard-luck mining town of Appalachia, Virginia, for example, are trying to capitalize on the fortuitous name of their town to create a useful fiction. "If we can create the myth of Appalachia being the past center of mountain life," the city manager explains, "then we can reap the benefits from the only thing we have to sell, the name Appalachia." Even as the real coal mines shut down and young people leave for elsewhere, the town plans to open an exhibition mine and offer certification attesting to visitors' identity as honorary Appalachians. Jeannie Ralston, "In the Heart of Appalachia," *National Geographic* (February 1993), 132.

10. The influential text in this regard is Eric Hobsbawm and Terrence Ranger, eds., *The Invention of Tradition* (New York: Cambridge University Press, 1983).

11. Doris Betts first presented such a list in "Many Souths and Broadening Scale: A Changing Southern Literature," in Dunn and Preston, eds., *The Future South*, 177–78.

12. John Egerton, *Shades of Gray: Dispatches from the Modern South* (Baton Rouge: Louisiana State University Press, 1991), 255–60.

13. James W. Fernandez, "Andalusia on Our Minds: Two Contrasting Places in Spain as Seen in a Vernacular Poetic Duel of the Late 19th Century," *Cultural Anthropology* 3 (1988), 21–35. Other interesting works in the new geography or new regionalism include: Appadurai, "Putting Hierarchy in Its Place"; J. Nicholas Entrikin, *The Betweenness of Place: Towards a Geography of Modernity* (Baltimore: Johns Hopkins University Press, 1991); Akhil Gupta and James Ferguson, "Beyond 'Culture': Space, Identity, and the Politics of Difference," *Cultural Anthropology* 7 (February 1992), 6–23; Liisa Malkki, "National Geographic: The Rooting of Peoples and the Territorialization of National Identity among Refugees and Scholars," *Cultural Anthropology* 7 (February 1992), 24–44. Especially useful is Allan Pred, *Making Histories and Constructing Human Geographies: The Local Transformation of Practice, Power Relations, and Consciousness* (Boulder, Colo.: Westview Press, 1990). Thomas Jefferson summarized these characteris-

tics in a famous letter to the Marquis de Chastellux, quoted in Garry Wills's *Inventing America: Jefferson's Declaration of Independence* (New York: Vintage Books, 1978), 283–84.

A survey of over three hundred undergraduates at the University of Virginia—young people from thirty-three different states, of diverse ethnicities, fewer than half of whom considered themselves Southerners—showed that the perception of Southern distinctiveness is alive and well. Of those who considered themselves Southerners, black and white, almost all declared themselves proud of that identity, with women and African Americans being the most likely to take pride in their regional background.

What, in these young people's eyes, set the South apart? Asked to rank twenty-eight attributes on a scale of Southernness, several traits consistently appeared at the top of the list. Speech, not surprisingly, struck almost everyone as different in the South. But beyond that, people commented most on the South's courtesy, hospitality, sense of history, and natural beauty. Black students and white had similar notions of what set the South apart except on one issue: African Americans ranked racism fourth while white students put racism in tenth place. These are very similar to the patterns found in the polls analyzed by John Shelton Reed. See n. 3 above.

Just about everyone I've casually queried, regardless of any regionality he or she may claim, agrees with this characterization of Southerners, black and white, as "nice." It seems to be perhaps the most tangible evidence of a Southern upbringing. Why? I think it may have had something to do originally with white people and black people forced to live together despite reasons for hatred on one side and fear on the other. Now it seems to be pursued for its own sake, a style that envelops and to some extent obscures other differences and conflicts. It can be put to the use of virtually any purpose, modern or antimodern.

14. William R. Taylor, *Cavalier and Yankee: The Old South and American National Character* (New York: George Braziller, 1960).

15. Sollors, *Beyond Ethnicity*, 190.

16. Michael Montgomery, "The Southern Accent—Alive and Well," *Southern Cultures* 1 (1993), 47–64.

17. Richard Graham, "Economics or Culture? The Development of the U.S. South and Brazil in the Days of Slavery," in Kees Gispen, ed., *What Made the South Different?* (Oxford: University of Mississippi Press, 1990).

18. In contrast, see A. Cash Koeniger, "Climate and Southern Distinctiveness," *Journal of Southern History* 54 (1988), 21–44.

19. For pioneering and exciting work in this vein, see Michael O'Brien, *Rethinking the South: Essays in Intellectual History* (Baltimore: Johns Hopkins University Press, 1988), 38–56. O'Brien's other works on Southern intellectual history develop these perspectives in extremely useful ways. See *The Idea of the American South, 1920–1941* (Baltimore: Johns Hopkins University Press, 1979) and *All Clever Men, Who Make Their Way: Critical Discourse in the Old South* (Fayetteville: University of Arkansas Press, 1982).

20. See Drew Gilpin Faust, *The Creation of Confederate Nationalism: Ideology and Identity in the Civil War South* (Baton Rouge: Louisiana State University Press, 1988).

21. Ibid., 10–11.

22. Colley, *Britons*, 5–6; Greenfeld, *Nationalism*, 476–77.

23. This point, among many others about the war, was made powerfully by Robert Penn Warren in his meditation *The Legacy of the Civil War* (New York: Random House, 1961).

24. Tracy Thompson, "The War between the States of Mind," *Washington Post*, January 10, 1993.

25. William Faulkner, *The Faulkner Reader* (New York: Random House, 1954), 315. I should like to thank Brad Mittendorf for calling this quote to my attention.

26. Pred, *Making Histories*.

27. Louis D. Rubin, Jr., *A Gallery of Southerners* (Baton Rouge: Louisiana State University Press, 1982), 206, 222.

A DIGITAL CIVIL WAR

1. For a thoughtful account of the beginnings of the institute (and much else), see Jerome McGann, *Radiant Textuality: Literature after the World Wide Web* (New York: Palgrave, 2001), 1–19.

2. See George P. Landow, *Hypertext 2.0: The Convergence of Contemporary Critical Theory and Technology* (Baltimore: Johns Hopkins University Press, 1997). The first version of Landow's book appeared in 1992.

3. Gary H. Anthes, "Technohumanities 101," *Computerworld* (February 1, 1993), 26.

4. Laurent Belsie, "The Electronic Village," *World Monitor: The Christian Science Monitor Monthly*, March 1993, 12–14.

5. http://jefferson.village.virginia.edu/vshadow/vshadow2.html.

6. http://jefferson.village.virginia.edu/staunton/intro.html.

7. *Charlottesville Daily Progress*, September 30, 1994, B1–2.

8. "Woodrow Wilson Birthplace 'History Harvest' reaps volumes of material," *Staunton Sunday News Leader*, October 2, 1994, A1, A2.

9. Edward L. Ayers and Anne Sarah Rubin, *The Valley of the Shadow—Eve of War* (New York: W. W. Norton and Company, 2000).

10. Landow, *Hypertext 2.0*, 183; Janet H. Murray, *Hamlet on the Holodeck: The Future of Narrative in Cyberspace* (New York: Free Press, 1997); Espen J. Aarseth, *Cybertext: Perspectives on Ergodic Literature* (Baltimore: Johns Hopkins University Press, 1997). An interesting attempt to build a book around multirelational text appears in Hans Ulrich Gumbrecht, *In 1926: Living at the Edge of Time* (Cambridge: Harvard University Press, 1997).

11. Robert Darnton, "A Program for Reviving the Monograph," *Perspectives* (March 1999), 25, 2.

12. Citation: Key =TAS9 in the article at http://www.vcdh.virginia.edu/AHR.

Worrying about the Civil War

1. Donald T. Phillips, *Lincoln on Leadership: Executive Strategies for Tough Times* (New York: Warner Books, 1992), 173. First published in 1992 and now in its eighth printing, the book bears rows of endorsements from prominent political figures, coaches, and corporate leaders. Bil Holton, *From Battlefield to Boardroom: The Leadership Lessons of Robert E. Lee* (Novato, Calif.: Presidio, 1995).

2. Michael Shaara, *The Killer Angels* (1974; paperback ed., New York: Ballantine, 1975); *Gettysburg*, a film directed by Ronald F. Maxwell, 1994.

3. James M. McPherson, *Battle Cry of Freedom: The Civil War Era* (New York: Oxford University Press, 1988); *The Civil War*, a nine-part documentary film directed by Ken Burns and shown by the Public Broadcasting System in 1990. McPherson has deepened and extended his interpretation in several books since *Battle Cry of Freedom*, including *Abraham Lincoln and the Second American Revolution* (New York: Oxford University Press, 1991), *What They Fought For, 1861–1865* (Baton Rouge: Louisiana State University Press, 1994), *Drawn with the Sword: Reflections on the American Civil War* (New York: Oxford University Press, 1996), and *For Cause and Comrades: Why Men Fought in the Civil War* (New York: Oxford University Press,

1997). McPherson's earlier overview of the era was called *Ordeal by Fire: The Civil War and Reconstruction* (New York: Alfred A. Knopf, 1982).

4. As a recent survey observes, Lincoln "now enjoys extremely high approval ratings"; older "doubts and reservations seem to have evaporated." Michael Perman, "Lincoln, the Civil War, and the New Approval Ratings," *American Studies* 36 (Spring 1995), 131–34. Penetrating comments on McPherson's interpretation appear in Michael Johnson, "Battle Cry of Freedom?," *Reviews in American History* 17 (June 1989), 214–18, and Jon L. Wakelyn's review of *Battle Cry of Freedom* in *Civil War History* 34 (December 1988), 344–47.

5. Burns's press kit for *The Civil War*, quoted in Jim Cullen, *Civil War in Popular Culture* (Washington, D.C.: Smithsonian Institution Press, 1995), 11; James McPherson, ed., *"We Cannot Escape History": Lincoln and the Last Best Hope of Earth* (Urbana and Chicago: University of Illinois Press, 1995), 12.

6. Geoffrey C. Ward, with Ric Burns and Ken Burns, *The Civil War: An Illustrated History* (New York: Alfred A. Knopf, 1990), xix. For stimulating and divergent discussions of the issues raised by Burns's series, see Robert Brent Toplin, ed., *Ken Burns's The Civil War: Historians Respond* (New York: Oxford University Press, 1996).

7. Edmund Wilson, *Patriotic Gore: Studies in the Literature of the American Civil War* (New York: Oxford University Press, 1962), xv–xix.

8. Robert Penn Warren, *The Legacy of the Civil War: Meditations on the Centennial* (New York: Random House, 1961), 64, 49–50.

9. Wilson, *Patriotic Gore*, xxxi. A blistering assessment of the Civil War from the perspective of the centennial also appears in Oscar Handlin, "The Civil War as Symbol and Actuality," *Massachusetts Review* 3 (Autumn 1961), 133–43.

10. Willie Lee Rose discusses the turn-of-the-century sectional compromise in *Race and Region in American Historical Fiction: Four Episodes in Popular Culture* (Oxford: Clarendon Press, 1979), 21–24.

11. Charles and Mary Beard, *The Rise of American Civilization* (New York: Macmillan, 1927), 51–54; Avery O. Craven, *The Repressible Conflict, 1830–1861* (Baton Rouge: Louisiana State University Press, 1939), 62–63.

For useful overviews, see Thomas J. Pressly, *Americans Interpret Their Civil War* (Princeton: Princeton University Press, 1954; 2nd ed., New York: Free Press, 1962); David Donald, "American Historians and the Causes of the Civil War," *South Atlantic Quarterly* 59 (Summer 1960), 351–55; David

M. Potter, "The Literature on the Background of the Civil War," in *The South and the Sectional Conflict* (Baton Rouge: Louisiana State University Press, 1968), 87–150; Peter Novick, *That Noble Dream: The "Objectivity Question" and the American Historical Profession* (Cambridge: Cambridge University Press, 1988), 72–80, 234–38, 354–59; Michael Perman, *The Coming of the American Civil War*, 3rd ed. (Lexington, Mass.: D. C. Heath, 1993).

12. James G. Randall, "The Blundering Generation," *Mississippi Valley Historical Review* 27 (June 1940), 3–28, quote on 18.

13. David W. Blight, " 'For Something beyond the Battlefield': Frederick Douglass and the Struggle for the Memory of the Civil War," *Journal of American History* 75 (March 1989), 1156–78; W. E. Burghardt DuBois, *Black Reconstruction: An Essay toward a History of the Part Which Black Folk Played in the Attempt to Reconstruct Democracy in America, 1860–1880* (New York: Russell and Russell, 1935), 714–16.

14. Arthur Schlesinger, Jr., "The Causes of the Civil War: A Note on Historical Sentimentalism," *Partisan Review* 16 (October 1949), 969–81, quotes on 980, 981; Benjamin Quarles, *The Negro in the Civil War* (Boston: Little, Brown and Company, 1953); Donald, "American Historians," 354. We can trace Craven's self-revisions in his *An Historian and the Civil War* (Chicago: University of Chicago Press, 1964).

15. Perhaps the most important book in this regard was Eric Foner's *Free Soil, Free Labor, Free Men: The Ideology of the Republican Party before the Civil War* (New York: Oxford University Press, 1970).

16. John S. Rosenberg, "Toward a New Civil War Revisionism," *The American Scholar* 38 (Spring 1969), 250–72, quote on 261; for the debate that ensued, see the response to Rosenberg in Phillip S. Paludan, "The American Civil War: Triumph through Tragedy," *Civil War History* 20 (September 1974), 239–50, and John S. Rosenberg, "The American Civil War and the Problem of 'Presentism': A Reply to Phillip S. Paludan," *Civil War History* 21 (September 1975), 242–53.

David M. Potter, while not an aggressive revisionist, wrote several brilliant essays that asked hard questions about comforting interpretations of the Civil War. They are collected in *The South and the Sectional Conflict*. While his posthumous and magisterial *The Impending Crisis, 1848–1861* (New York: Harper and Row, 1976) cannot be clearly labeled, Potter's revisionist leanings are clear in a textbook, *Divisions and the Stresses of Union, 1845–1876* (Glenview, Ill.: Scott, Foresman, 1973).

17. For an influential statement of this argument, see Eric Foner, "The Causes

of the American Civil War: Recent Interpretations and New Directions," *Civil War History* 20 (September 1974), 197–214.

18. Burns: "If you see history like the life of a human being, this [the Civil War] was the traumatic event of our childhood." *Newsweek* (October 8, 1990), 59. McPherson, *Lincoln and the Second American Revolution*, 13.

19. *Glory*, a film directed by Edward Zwick, 1989. Ironically, Warren served on Burns's team of advisers and is quoted in the introduction to the book based on the series (xix). Burns focuses on Warren's statement that the war was so central and complex event that it tends to create a personal connection to Americans. In many ways, though, Burns's *Civil War* seems an example of the sentimental nationalism Warren warned against thirty years earlier.

20. McPherson, *Battle Cry of Freedom*, 858; Thomas Cripps, "Historical Truth: An Interview with Ken Burns," *American Historical Review* 100 (June 1995), 741–64. Hannah Arendt, *On Violence* (New York: Harcourt, Brace and World, 1970), paraphrased in Jean Bethke Elshtain, "Reflections on War and Political Discourse: Realism, Just War, and Feminism in a Nuclear Age," Elshtain, *Just War Theory* (Oxford: Blackwell, 1992), 260–79, quote on 270.

21. First quote from James M. McPherson, *The Negro's Civil War: How American Negroes Felt and Acted during the War for the Union* (New York: Pantheon, 1965), 34. The second quote is in Garry Wills, *Lincoln at Gettysburg: The Words that Remade America* (New York: Simon & Schuster, 1992), 38–39.

22. Wills, *Lincoln at Gettysburg*, 37–39, 183–85. David Brion Davis has explored, with characteristic subtlety, the conflation of Lincoln with the images associated with individual emancipation. See his "The Emancipation Moment," in Gabor S. Boritt, ed., *Lincoln, the War President* (New York: Oxford University Press, 1992), 63–88.

23. Potter, *Impending Crisis*; J. Mill Thornton III, *Politics and Power in a Slave Society: Alabama, 1800–1860* (Baton Rouge: Louisiana State University Press, 1978); Michael F. Holt, *The Political Crisis of the 1850s* (New York: Wiley, 1978) and *Political Parties and American Political Development from the Age of Jackson to the Age of Lincoln* (Baton Rouge: Louisiana State University Press, 1992); William E. Gienapp, *The Origins of the Republican Party, 1852–1856* (New York: Oxford University Press, 1986); William W. Freehling, *The Road to Disunion: The Secessionists at Bay* (New York: Oxford University Press, 1990) and *The Reintegration of American History: Slavery and the Civil War* (New York: Oxford University Press, 1994).

24. On blacks' efforts to strike their freedom, see Armstead Robinson, *Bitter*

Fruits of Bondage: The Demise of Slavery and the Collapse of the Confederacy, 1861–1865 (Charlottesville, Va.: University of Virginia Press, 2004); Ira Berlin, Barbara J. Fields, Thavolia Glymph, Joseph P. Reidy, and Leslie Rowland, eds., *Freedom: A Documentary History of Emancipation, 1861–1867* ser. 1, vol. 1 (New York: Cambridge University Press, 1985), and Leon F. Litwack, *Been in the Storm So Long: The Aftermath of Slavery* (New York: Alfred A. Knopf, 1979). For strong criticism of Burns on this issue, see Litwack, "Telling the Story: The Historian, the Filmmaker, and the Civil War," in Toplin, ed., *Ken Burns's The Civil War*, 119–40.

25. Michael Perman, *The Road to Redemption: Southern Politics, 1869–1879* (Chapel Hill: University of North Carolina Press, 1984), Michael Fellman, *Inside War: The Guerrilla Conflict in Missouri during the American Civil War* (New York: Oxford University Press, 1989), Charles Royster, *The Destructive War: William Tecumseh Sherman, Stonewall Jackson, and the Americans* (New York: Alfred A. Knopf, 1991), Fellman, *Citizen Sherman: A Life of William Tecumseh Sherman* (New York: Random House, 1995), and Stephen V. Ash, *When the Yankees Came: Conflict and Chaos in the Occupied South, 1861–1865* (Chapel Hill: University of North Carolina Press, 1995).

26. A counterargument that has received McPherson's endorsement is Mark Grimsley, *The Hard Hand of War: Union Military Policy toward Southern Civilians, 1861–1865* (Cambridge: Cambridge University Press, 1995).

27. Battlefield contingency is the major analytical argument in McPherson's *Battle Cry of Freedom*, where he posits four points at which the North could have lost the war. See 857–58.

28. McPherson makes this point explicitly in *Ordeal by Fire*, 13, and implicitly in *Battle Cry of Freedom*; Kenneth C. Davis, *Don't Know Much about the Civil War: Everything You Need to Know about America's Greatest Conflict but Never Learned* (New York: Morrow, 1996), 151–52; George Fredrickson, "Blue over Gray: Sources of Success and Failure in the Civil War," in Fredrickson, ed., *A Nation Divided: Problems and Issues of the Civil War and Reconstruction* (Minneapolis: Burgess, 1975), 78.

29. Richard Graham, "Economics or Culture? The Development of the U.S. South and Brazil in the Days of Slavery," in Kees Gispen, ed., *What Made the South Different?* (Oxford: University of Mississippi Press, 1990). For insightful portrayals of "modern" influences in the South, see Thornton, *Politics and Power*, Eugene D. Genovese, *The Slaveholders' Dilemma: Freedom and Progress in Southern Conservative Thought, 1820–1860* (Columbia: University of South Carolina Press, 1992), and Kenneth W. Noe, *Southwest*

Virginia's Railroad: Modernization and the Sectional Crisis (Urbana: University of Illinois Press, 1994).

30. A recent magisterial history puts it well: The Old South was "not premodern but deeply implicated in modernity, though an idiosyncratic version mostly based on slavery." Michael O'Brien, *Conjectures of Order: Intellectual Life and the American South, 1810–1860* (Chapel Hill: University of North Carolina Press, 2004), vol. 1, p. 17. Jeffrey Rogers Hummel offers iconoclastic and penetrating commentary on the war in his book, *Emancipating Slaves, Enslaving Free Men: A History of the American Civil War* (Chicago: Open Court, 1996). Hummel, from the viewpoint of one who finds the market and its values more just and efficient than those of the state, challenges some of the orthodoxies of the liberal interpretation. He argues that a war for union alone was not the worthy crusade it often appears: "As an excuse for civil war, maintaining the State's territorial integrity is bankrupt and reprehensible" (352). Hummel believes that the war was not the only, or even the best, way of ending slavery, pointing out that the amount of money the North alone spent on the war "was enough to buy all slaves and set up each family with forty acres and a mule" (354). The source of his dissent, reflected in his title, is that "in contrast to the whittling away of government that had preceded Fort Sumter, the United States had commenced its halting but inexorable march toward the welfare-warfare State of today" (359). Hummel's notes on the historical literature are often biting, but his narrative of the war's coming, fighting, and aftermath does not differ markedly from more conventional accounts. His political perspective has revealed to him the evasions and conventions of the current orthodoxy and suggested promising areas for further reflection and research, but he has not yet offered a coherent counternarrative of the conflict. For an interesting overview of recent writing on the Civil War from the right, see Daniel Feller, "Libertarians in the Attic, or A Tale of Two Narratives," *Reviews in American History* 32 (June 2004), 184–95.

WHAT CAUSED THE CIVIL WAR?

1. On *The Simpsons*, see the transcript for the episode "Much Apu about Nothing," written by David S. Cohen and directed by Susie Dietter, Production Code: 3F20, Original Airdate in N.A.: 5-May-96, Capsule revision C, 10-Jun-96, in "The Simpsons Archive" on the World Wide Web: http://www.snpp.com/. I am grateful to Scot French for calling this episode to my attention.

2. See Gary J. Kornblith, "Rethinking the Coming of the Civil War: A Counterfactual Exercise," *Journal of American History* 90 (June 2003), 76–105. Kornblith offers a useful survey of the literature on the issue.

3. See, for example, James M. McPherson, *Battle Cry of Freedom: The Civil War Era* (New York: Oxford University Press, 1988), 255, and William W. Freehling, *The South vs. the South: How Anti-Confederate Southerners Shaped the Course of the Civil War* (New York: Oxford University Press, 2001), 22–24.

4. For a thoughtful and helpful overview of this literature, see Daniel W. Crofts, *Reluctant Confederates: Upper South Unionists in the Secession Crisis* (Chapel Hill: University of North Carolina Press, 1989). The local bases of politics in Virginia have been portrayed in Crofts, *Old Southampton: Politics and Society in a Virginia County, 1834–1869* (Charlottesville: University Press of Virginia, 1992); the complexities of its state-level politics appear in William G. Shade, *Democratizing the Old Dominion: Virginia and the Second Party System, 1824–1861* (Charlottesville: University Press of Virginia, 1996).

5. In addition to the books described in "Worrying about the Civil War" in this volume, the issue of modernity is analyzed in considerable detail in the digital article prepared by William G. Thomas III and myself: "The Differences Slavery Made: A Close Analysis of Two American Communities," *American Historical Review* 108 (December 2003): 1298–1307 and http://www.vcdh.virginia.edu/AHR. In addition to the works discussed there, see Beth Barton Schweiger, *The Gospel Working Up: Progress and the Pulpit in Nineteenth-Century Virginia* (New York: Oxford University Press, 2000); Michael O'Brien, *Conjectures of Order: Intellectual Life and the American South, 1810–1860* (Chapel Hill: University of North Carolina Press, 2004); James Huston, *Calculating the Value of the Union: Slavery, Property Rights, and the Economic Origins of the Civil War* (Chapel Hill: University of North Carolina Press, 2003), 24–66; and Peter Carmichael, *The Last Generation: Young Virginians in Peace, War, and Reunion* (Chapel Hill: University of North Carolina Press, 2005).

6. A stimulating and innovative account that emphasizes the modernity of the Confederacy is Drew Gilpin Faust, *The Creation of Confederate Nationalism: Ideology and Identity in the Civil War South* (Baton Rouge: Louisiana State University Press, 1989). On the projection of boundaries in time, see Peter S. Onuf, "Federalism, Republicanism, and the Origins of American Sectionalism," in Edward L. Ayers, Patricia Nelson Limerick, Stephen Nissenbaum, and Peter S. Onuf, *All over the Map: Rethinking American Regions* (Baltimore: Johns Hopkins University Press, 1996). On

the South's self-image, see Michael O'Brien, *Conjectures of Order: Intellectual Life and the American South, 1810–1860* (Chapel Hill: University of North Carolina Press, 2004). Any explanation has to begin with the acknowledgment that all white Southerners possessed an enormous and rational economic interest in the institution. James Huston has demonstrated that property in enslaved people accounted for almost 19 percent of all the nation wealth in 1860 and that American slaves were worth more than American railroads and manufacturing combined. Ranked by wealth per capita for the white population, the slave states were the richest in the United States; even the poorest slaveholding state, North Carolina, ranked ahead of New York, Pennsylvania, and Ohio. Huston, *Calculating the Value of the Union*, 65.

7. W. E. B. DuBois, *Black Reconstruction: An Essay Toward a History of the Part Which Black Folk Played in the Attempt to Reconstruct Democracy in America, 1800–1860* (New York: Russell and Russell, 1935), 715.

8. This is the argument of one of the most influential books to appear in recent years in the social sciences: Benedict Anderson, *Imagined Communities: Reflections on the Origin and Spread of Nationalism* (rev. and extended ed., London: Verso, 1991).

By 1860 the United States had 3,725 newspapers with an annual circulation of nearly 888 million copies—up from 186.5 million copies in 1840. The number of telegraph miles in service went from 0 to 50,000 in those twenty years, and the number of railroad miles increased from 2,818 to 36,626. Lorman A. Ratner and Dwight L. Teeter, Jr., *Fanatics and Fire-Eaters: Newspapers and the Coming of the Civil War* (Urbana: University of Illinois Press, 2003), 9, 18.

9. Important books that emphasize the dynamics of the political system itself in bringing on the Civil War include Michael F. Holt, *The Political Crisis of the 1850s* (New York: Wiley, 1978) and *Political Parties and American Political Development from the Age of Jackson to the Age of Lincoln* (Baton Rouge: Louisiana State University Press, 1992); William E. Gienapp, *The Origins of the Republican Party, 1852–1856* (New York: Oxford University Press, 1986); William W. Freehling, *The Road to Disunion: The Secessionists at Bay* (New York: Oxford University Press, 1990) and *The Reintegration of American History: Slavery and the Civil War* (New York: Oxford University Press, 1994).

10. Stephen Kern, *A Cultural History of Causality: Science, Murder Novels, and Systems of Thought* (Princeton: Princeton University Press, 2004), 6.

EXPORTING RECONSTRUCTION

1. For a useful overview, see Tony Smith's *America's Mission: The United States and the Worldwide Struggle for Democracy in the Twentieth Century* (Princeton: Princeton University Press, 1994).

2. For a powerful account of the role of Reconstruction in the twentieth century, see Grace Elizabeth Hale, *Making Whiteness: The Culture of Segregation in the South, 1890–1940* (New York: Pantheon, 1998), pp. 43–84; On *Beloved*, see Robert Jackson, *The Gilded Land: Seeking the Region in American Literature and Culture* (Baton Rouge: Louisiana State University Press, 2005).

   The old story of Reconstruction still appeals, as attested to by the critically acclaimed release of *Gone with the Wind* in a four-DVD boxed set with subtitles in three languages, Dolby sound, footage from the 1939 Atlanta premiere and the 1961 Civil War Centennial, and a theatrical short from 1940, *The Old South*.

3. Quoted in Hale, *Making Whiteness*, p. 81.

4. Eric Foner, *Reconstruction: America's Unfinished Revolution, 1863–1877* (New York: Harper and Row, 1988).

5. See Steven Hahn, "Class and State in Postemancipation Societies: Southern Planters in Comparative Perspective," *American Historical Review* 95 (February 1990), pp., 75–98.

6. Quoted in Smith, *America's Mission*, p. 3.

7. In Ira Berlin, et al., *Free at Last: A Documentary History of Slavery, Freedom, and the Civil War* (New York: New Press, 1992), pp. 497–505.

8. Quoted in Smith, *America's Mission*, p. 81.

9. Wolfgang Schivelbusch, *The Culture of Defeat: On National Trauma, Mourning, and Recovery* (New York: Metropolitan Books, 2003; translated by Jefferson Chase from the German edition, published in 2001), pp. 1–35. For excellent discussions of these dynamics, also see Nina Silber, *The Romance of Reunion: Northerners and the South, 1865–1900* (Chapel Hill: University of North Carolina Press, 1993) and Anne Sarah Rubin, *A Shattered Nation: The Rise and Fall of the Confederacy, 1861–1868* (Chapel Hill: University of North Carolina Press, 2005).

10. For a rich portrayal of this complicated and contentious process, see David W. Blight, *Race and Reunion: The Civil War in American Memory* (Cambridge: Harvard University Press, 2001).

11. John W. Dower, *Embracing Defeat: Japan in the Wake of World War II* (New York: W. W. Norton, 1999), pp. 525–26. In post–World War II Germany

too, shades of American Reconstruction hovered. Lucius Clay, leader of the American occupation, had grown up in Georgia. He said in a meeting that he was "going to be damn sure that there weren't any carpetbaggers in the military government; that no one, if I could help it, was going to make an exorbitant profit out of Germany's defeat." Reporters, Clay recalled, immediately determined that "I'd been influenced by my background. Maybe I had." Jean Edward Smith, *Lucius C. Clay: An American Life* (New York: Henry Holt, 1990), p. 239.

12. Tony Smith, who has surveyed the efforts by the United States to foster democratic states over the last century, finds that "the genius, and also the tragedy" of American policies have been their ability to be "genuinely innovative politically" but not "profoundly settling socioeconomically." Established elites could adapt to democracy if they would, especially in developed societies, such as Japan and Germany. But in countries that were predominantly agricultural, American policies did not do "enough to create the cultural, economic, and social circumstances that could reinforce a democratic political order." Thus "American efforts failed completely" in Central America and the Caribbean during Woodrow Wilson's presidency or "created narrowly based and highly corrupt elitist forms of democracy" in the Philippines and in the Dominican Republic. See Smith, *America's Mission*, p. 18.

13. Quoted in Foner, *Reconstruction*, p. 235.

14. See Mark W. Summers, *Railroads, Reconstruction, and the Gospel of Prosperity: Aid under the Radical Republicans, 1865–1877* (Princeton: Princeton University Press, 1984) and J. Mills Thornton III, "Fiscal Policy and the Failure of Radical Reconstruction in the Lower South," in *Region, Race, and Reconstruction: Essays in Honor of C. Vann Woodward*, J. Morgan Kousser and James M. McPherson, ed. (New York: Oxford University Press, 1982).

15. C. Vann Woodward, *The Burden of Southern History*, rev. ed. (New York: Mentor, 1968), p. 148.

TELLING THE STORY OF THE NEW SOUTH

1. W. J. Cash, *The Mind of the South* (New York: Alfred A. Knopf, 1941).

2. Ibid., 200, 201.

3. Ibid., 237, 229.

4. James Agee, *Let Us Now Praise Famous Men* (Boston: Houghton Mifflin, 1941), 7.

5. C. Vann Woodward, *Tom Watson: Agrarian Rebel* (New York: Macmillan, 1938); *Origins of the New South, 1877–1913* (Baton Rouge: Louisiana State University Press, 1951); *The Strange Career of Jim Crow* (New York: Oxford University Press, 1955).

6. C. Vann Woodward, *Thinking Back: The Perils of Writing History* (Baton Rouge: Louisiana State University Press, 1986), 55.

7. Woodward to Virginia Durr, June 8, 1952, quoted in Morton Sosna, *In Search of the Silent South: Southern Liberals and the Race Issue* (New York: Columbia University Press, 1977), 11.

8. William B. Hesseltine, review of *Origins of the New South, American Historical Review* 57 (July 1952), 993–94.

9. Edward L. Ayers, *The Promise of the New South: Life after Reconstruction* (New York: Oxford University Press, 1992); Howard N. Rabinowitz, "Origins of a Poststructural New South: A Review of Edward L. Ayers's *The Promise of the New South: Life after Reconstruction*," *Journal of Southern History* LIX (August 1993), 505–15.

10. A number of books that might be considered open in various ways have been published in Southern history, pioneered by Rhys Isaac's *Transformation of Virginia, 1740–1790* (Chapel Hill: University of North Carolina Press, 1982). Other examples of what I take to be, for various reasons, open narratives include Michael P. Johnson and James L. Roark, *Black Masters: A Free Family of Color in the Old South* (New York: W. W. Norton, 1984); Suzanne Lebsock, *The Free Women of Petersburg: Status and Culture in a Southern Town, 1784–1860* (New York: W. W. Norton, 1984); Theodore Rosengarten, *Tombee: Portrait of a Cotton Planter* (New York: Morrow, 1986); Allen Tullos, *Habits of Industry: White Culture and the Transformation of the Carolina Piedmont* (Chapel Hill: University of North Carolina Press, 1989); Melton Alonza McLaurin, *Celia, a slave* (Athens: University of Georgia Press, 1991); Winthrop D. Jordan, *Tumult and Silence at Second Creek: An Inquiry into a Civil War Slave Conspiracy* (Baton Rouge: Louisiana State University Press, 1993); and James Goodman, *Stories of Scottsboro* (New York: Pantheon, 1994). None of these authors have been asked to give their endorsement to the views put forward in this essay, which focuses on motives that I infer from their books. Notice that "open" does not mean "inclusive"; there have been many social histories of the South that include a wide range of people and evidence that speak from a relatively "fixed" point of view. As the remainder of the essay suggests, I do not intend that as a criticism.

Each experimental narrative is open in a different way. Taking his cue from the anthropologist Clifford Geertz, for example, Rhys Isaac dwells on the way ritual, landscape, and presentation of self dramatized the deep structures of power in colonial Virginia. For Isaac, history is not so much a stream from one event to another as it is a series of juxtapositions, a series of "resonances" created among simultaneous processes. His narrative takes the form of a series of tableaux vivants, of dramas played out by actors half conscious of their roles. The narratives of Lebsock, Rosengarten, McLaurin, and Jordan, on the other hand, focus on close interpretations of ambiguous documents, piecing together motive and consequence. The haunting story of black masters told by Johnson and Roark begins with a box of old letters found under a porch; the narrative continually calls attention to the inferences made from those letters, the things left unsaid in the record. In Allen Tullos's book, in some ways the boldest of the open narrativists, one chapter consists almost entirely of an uninterrupted and uninterpreted transcript of a woman's oral account of her life. Goodman's history of Scottsboro calls attention to the margins of the story, to the long days in prison or on parole, as well as to public events. His very title stresses that "Scottsboro" was not so much one story as many, not so much a single event as the intersection of disparate lives. I discuss Goodman's open narratives in "Prisms and Prisons," *New Republic* 211 (July 11, 1994), 36–38.

11. Robert J. Norrell, "The Way They Were," *Virginia Quarterly Review* 69 (Summer 1993), 551–55.

12. Reinhold Niebuhr, *The Children of Light and the Children of Darkness* (New York: Charles Scribner's Sons, 1944); C. Vann Woodward, *The Burden of Southern History* (Baton Rouge: Louisiana State University Press, 1960).

INDEX

Marx, Karl, 56
Mason-Dixon Line, 66, 67
Maxwell, Ronald F., 198n
memex, 76
Mencken, H. L., 172
Methodists, 54
Mexico, U.S. war with, 53
military history, 116
Mind of the South, The (Cash), 168–70,
    171, 172
minstrel shows, 15
Mitchell, Margaret, 171
Mittendorf, Brad, 197n
modernization, antebellum trends
    of, 125–28, 138–42, 203n,
    204n
Molly Hatchett, 37, 193n
Morrison, Toni, 146
Mosaic, 80
Mullins, Michael, 86
music, 18–19, 20, 43, 46, 47, 96,
    193n

narratives, fixed vs. open, 176–81,
    208n–9n
NASCAR, 18, 46
Nashville Agrarians, 170
National Archives, 86
National Endowment for the
    Humanities, 85
nationalist movements, 55–57,
    58–59
Negro in the Civil War, The (Quarles),
    114
Nelson, Ted, 77
Netherlands, 95–101
    American cultural influence in, 96,
        97, 98–100
    regional tensions within, 98

in slave trade, 95, 97
in World War II, 100–101
New Orleans, La., tourist imagery
    of, 99
new social history, 68
New South, 69, 167–81
    economic growth of, 187
    open narratives of, 176–81,
        208n–9n
    political leaders of, 171, 172–73,
        175, 180
    power categories of, 178–79
    segregation in, 10, 175
newspapers, 139, 140, 141, 167,
    205n
Niebuhr, Reinhold, 181

O'Brien, Michael, 197n, 203n
Office of Scientific Research and
    Development, 75
open narratives, 176–81, 208n–9n
Ordeal by Fire (McPherson), 199n,
    202n
Order of the Arrow, 16
Origins of the New South (Woodward),
    30, 171–72, 173, 174, 180,
    181
Oxford Book of the American South, The,
    100

Paludan, Phillip S., 200n
panic of 1873, 163
Paper Chase, The, 27
Parton, Dolly, 20
party politics, 136–38, 139, 142
Patriotic Gore (Wilson), 110
Pennsylvanians, Civil War experiences of, 67
Percy, Walker, 47